THE
MIND
FACTORY

*The Ability to Cipher Information
is a Secret of the Lexicon*

LARRY ODELL JOHNSON

INKS&
BINDINGS

INKS &
BINDINGS

Inks and Bindings
888-290-5218
www.inksandbindings.com
orders@inksandbindings.com

CONTENTS

I dedicate this book to Africans and to all descendants of African slaves.

PREFACE

The content of the following book represents a study under the branch of sociology known as the Sociology of Knowledge. Within those parameters, much of what I have delineated in this book is very explicit. What the above statements translate into is that I have a lot I feel needs to be said about our everyday reality, and although I say it using a sociological perspective, I believe I have succeeded in saying it in everyday terms. The very nature of this form and level of communication necessitates that while much is explicitly expressed, there are additionally many things that are merely implied in what I have written. This feature is characteristic of the *levels* of understanding that are inherent in my book, and as one will discover from this reading, implication is generally a prescribed feature of all language and symbolism. Moreover, since I decided that certain things were better left unstated, the more that is implied in my book is both by necessity and by design. There are an unavoidable *small* amount of invectives in the book. They are not included to offend anyone, and as used and explained within limited and meaningful contexts, I am confident the reader will not be offended. More importantly, the reader will discover that the profane words used are an integral part of this commentary. That is, this book is poised to illustrate that all language, even its seemingly repugnant forms, has well-defined and relevant intent. What is interesting is that this book reveals certain intellectual and social contents that do not contain invectives but that some could yet find offensive. The bottom line is that my book is not designed to shield its reader from reality but, rather, to expose its reader more intimately to what *is*—even if reluctantly—reality. In addition, the book contains a large set of anagrams whose overall content appreciation demands that they be considered as a group. My goal is to promote the use and normalization of anagrams as a necessary and sufficient technique in the cryptographic interpretation of text.

Chapter 1 is uniquely expository, yet at the same time, it is also intended to act as a hook. I quite frankly hoped to excite the reader's curiosity. Chapter 1 was not initially the first chapter. I reshuffled the chapters to make the book more of the *tool* I hope it to be.

Chapter 2 is expository, but at the same time, I needed to lay the theoretical foundation for the subsequent chapters. With regard to the idea of laying a foundation, I have also occasionally embedded parenthetical biblical quotations within the text. These quotations are to be read as part of the ongoing discussion. However, the *parenthetical* quotations can be ignored without loss of continuity. Although this is not a book about religion, I thought it imperative that the reader understand that science and religion—like science and art—are inextricably interwoven. As a result, some of the textual ideas are by necessity slightly repetitive. Nonetheless, I have additionally included extended bracketed commentary within what might be an unusually large number of quotations. In fact, all but two or three of the bracketed comments in this book are my own, and it is typically quite obvious where they are mine. It has been my intention and tactic to use bracketed commentary within directed quotes because they are effective in restricting the length of this volume. I wanted to avoid the typical situation where books of this type can read far too slowly and be very tedious as well. Consequently, unlike the parenthetical notes, the bracketed commentary *must* be read to appreciate the overall content and meaning in the book.

Chapters 3 and 4 represent the theoretical core of the book, with chapter 4 being the intended centerpiece of the book. I use chapter 3 merely to explain what is actually being discussed in Kant's *Critique of Pure Reason*.[1] While chapter 3 discusses Kant's *Critique*, chapter 4 looks at examples presumably of the type that Kant rejected, arguing that general examples can be given in a meaningful way and that examples are essential to a full understanding of Kant's discussion. The examples take the form of anagrams. Thus chapter 4 is additionally designed to put the development of anagrams on a systematic and scientific footing, and places anagrams firmly and formally within the public domain where it can now be *known* that the kind of information anagrams can provide has openly, yet surreptitiously, existed all along. Finally, I use the anagrams in chapter 4 as a tool to expose some of my personal knowledge with regard to information technology's *content* and reveal how much of the philosophical underpinnings of language I personally understand. I do so because, while avoiding a more lengthy discussion, I want to make my *view* into these matters as clear as is reasonably possible. Chapter 4 will thus serve as a benchmark for those who already have insight into these matters, of how much I have been willing to discuss and how much I have not been willing to reveal in this book. And what is more important, it is done for the purpose of encouraging potential future authors on these matters to *also* find it unnecessary to permit their public discussions to degenerate into what could quite easily be considered too politically sensitive or inappropriate public revelations on content.

Chapter 5, along with earlier biblical quotations inserted into the text, is used to acknowledge the important and immediately relevant substance of the Bible. It emphasizes the role that biblical substance plays in our everyday lives, as well as suggesting the Bible's significance in informing our understanding of the stock of knowledge under discussion.

As a result of having had so much intellectual ground to cover in a book of limited length, I feel I have not been able to give adequate coverage to, and thus appreciation to, establishing just how intimately we as human beings are all spiritually connected. I view reality as connecting each of us through language as the earthly representative and embodiment of the Holy Spirit. Additionally, I have wanted to imply that it is just as valuable to learn from doing something as it is to learn how to do something. In other words, practice is just as essential to theory as theory is to practice. Of course, the combination of practice and theory is much bigger than the sum of its parts. In the end, it is often of practical importance for one to learn as much as possible about a subject before actually undertaking the formal study of that subject. And that is a stream of thought that is consistent with, and is the *practical* significance of, a *priori* knowledge or pre-suppositional thinking. This fact is especially true for the educationally disadvantaged students of formal academic disciplines. The reason being that learning as learning alone is mostly a social- psychological phenomenon; however, the acquisition of academic credentials is primarily a sociopolitical and economic reality. That is, and I am only speaking within an American context, the young can readily be nurtured into a sincere willingness and desire to do their best to *learn* as much as they can in order to be the best that they can be in society. Witness, for example, how the young often response energetically and positively to the question of what they want to be when they grow up. However, apart from the natural activity of one simply changing his/her mind about an original career goal, the cost of higher education for the average person born into poverty can be prohibitive. If one combines the reality of economic hardship with the historically inherent institutional and intensely active racial bias—together with the *traditional* gender bias—in our educational systems along with employment discrimination, the result is predictable and self-evident. Under the above given circumstances, one should be able to understand how some of the best efforts of the *innocent* to persevere, and succeed to the point where they achieve their original career goals, are typically undermined and their goals are often thwarted. Most significantly, I am acknowledging and suggesting to persons on the street, who are already in full possession of the basic elements of the wisdom that I am uncovering in this book, that it is a practical wisdom. And it is a level of understanding that is far superior to and often beyond the typical imagination of many of us who have gained our wisdom primarily by formal academic means.

I have personalized some of my above comments and some of the content of the book because major aspects of this book are thoroughly *autobiographical* in nature. My outlook and opinions have been honed by lived experiences that are intimately related to what is being discussed. Moreover, the content is dear to me with regards to the extent to which it encompasses my life's work, so far. Although I have some amorphous ideas for several related and several "unrelated" additional books, even if I never get the opportunity to complete another work, I feel satisfied and privileged in having been able to make this one formally bold and definitive contribution to our everyday stock of knowledge.

I know of no single book that single-handedly can ever eliminate all of the blind spots in one's understanding that is brought on by one's natural birthright into the lack of a completely functional understanding of the affairs of his/her everyday world. However, I also know that my personal understanding of the facts of life in general has been greatly enhanced by my being repeatedly reminded and learning to "appreciate"—with each new increment of greater understanding—that I really know very little with respect to the total scheme of things. I hope that my little book will give its readers an understanding of the power that I feel is inherent in this kind of appreciation.[2] Learning is a wonderfully endless journey.

Lastly, I wish to express my deepest heartfelt appreciation to those relatively few very dear friends and relatives, whose names I will not mention because they know who they are, who have believed in me, encouraged me, and stood by me through even the harshest of life experiences. To the extent this book will be honored, I am indebted to each of you.

ENDNOTES

1   There are three principal reasons why Kant's *Critique* is important to me. The first reason is because, although tedious, it is well written. Second, his theory lends support to what I have previously discovered through research into the origin of language, linguistic theory, and cryptographic interpretation of text. Third, his perspective is an excellent example of a particular intellectual tradition. I will have more to say about that tradition when I discuss Kant's work at length. It is an intellectual tradition whose posturizing I am convinced needed to be uncovered.

2   See David Matza's book, *Becoming Deviant*, for an invaluable discussion and a definitive understanding of the sense in which I am using the term "appreciation." In reviewing that material, one will additionally gain insight into why Matza's book is among the relatively few books that I consider as masterpieces in sociology.

CHAPTER ONE

WHAT MORE DID ALBERT EINSTEIN KNOW?

Wisdom is the principal thing; therefore, get wisdom; and with all thy getting, get understanding.

—Prov. 4: 7

The goal of this book is to explore some of the most complex elements of human knowledge and, in the process, to gain some mastery of what is there waiting to be understood. There can be no doubt that the world we live in is very complex; therefore— while negotiating our way in the world—prudence would suggest we should choose not to avoid the complex, but rather, to embrace the complex and to find what simplicity lies within it. In this sense, my book is purely exposition. That is, my intent is to use description and explanation to expose certain truths which will enable the reader to make more informed life choices as a consequence of having been exposed to a wider range of facts about our everyday taken-for-granted reality. In this effort, the complex cannot be made simple; yet, however, this book is testament to the fact that when the reader is appropriately assisted, complex literature can be understood. In that regard, I believe I have accomplished something quite unusual with this book. And on this point, I hope you, the reader, will eventually conclude that you have no option other than to agree.

In order to elucidate some of the subtleties of meaning in this

1

exposition, it will first be necessary to focus some brief attention on the work of two major modern-day theorists: Albert Einstein and Sigmund Freud. My purpose in using some of Einstein's written work and some of Freud's written work is to illustrate their unique contributions to the levels of understanding I am referencing in my book. As it has turned out, despite the common opinion that the work of these two theorists is too difficult to understand, their contributions to the general "stock of knowledge" (Berger and Luckmann, 1966) yields for us the most direct insight into the complex literature I am reviewing in my book. Without their contributions, my task would likely have been much more difficult. Moreover, in deference to the everyday reader who I am trying to reach, the reader will experience being able to observe the pointed insight—of at least these two theorists—without getting into an extended or drawn-out analysis of major portions of their work. Although the contents of their respective theories are ostensibly unrelated, the combined effect of their contributions have helped to inform my own awareness and understanding of what and how to access that *something* which lay behind the veil. This is a veil more commonly known to the everyday person as formal and conventional knowledge.

One of the biggest names in the history of modern science is Albert Einstein. Of course, he is best known for his theory of relativity. Yet few know him for the profound philosopher that he was. There can be no doubt that he was a great physicist, but some of his most poignant work came in the form of his philosophical commentary. We shall begin our journey with a quote attributed to Albert Einstein (1956), which influenced a qualitative change in the way I personally have come to view knowledge. As he so eloquently—if not poetically—states:

> The fairest thing we can experience is the mysterious. It
> is the fundamental emotion, which stands at the cradle of
> true art and true science. He who knows it not and can no
> longer wonder, no longer feel amazement, is as good as dead,

a snuffed-out candle. It was the experience of mystery—even if mixed with fear—that engendered religion. A knowledge of the existence of something we cannot penetrate, of the manifestations of the profoundest reason and the most radiant beauty, which are only accessible to our reason in their most elementary forms—it is this knowledge and this emotion that constitute the truly religious attitude; in this sense, and in this alone, I am a deeply religious man. I cannot conceive of a God who rewards and punishes his creatures, or has a will of the type of which we are conscious in ourselves. An individual who should survive his physical death is also beyond my comprehension, nor do I wish it otherwise; such notions are for the fears or absurd egoism of feeble souls. Enough for me the mystery of the eternity of life, and the inkling of the marvelous structure of reality, together with the single-hearted endeavor to comprehend a portion, be it never so tiny, of the reason that manifests itself in nature (ibid., p. 5).[1]

One must pause for a moment and meditate on Einstein's words before he/she truly begins to appreciate the depth of the insight this great scientist is exposing to his readers. Einstein is suggesting that a person can reach a point in his/her intellectual development where he/she is *emotionally* affected by their desire and effort to understand things that are not easily explained. He is additionally suggesting that individuals can benefit from having had this kind of emotional experience. That is, at the level of an emotion, the mysterious—things that are puzzling—stimulates the search for answers and results in a tremendous amount of learning. Moreover, let me immediately state, from the standpoint of a cipher, the above quotation is replete with information and meaning which can be systematically elaborated upon.[2] However, it is not my purpose to explain the cipher contained in this immediate quote. For the moment, I wish simply to point out why this quote was instrumental in stimulating me to actively focus on and puzzle over what I suspected had a much deeper meaning and to even anticipate that it potentially contained a cipher.

I do not recall the exact point when I first read the above quote by Albert Einstein. No matter, at some point while doing research on the Sociology of Knowledge, I stumbled onto the subject of cryptography. In studying some of those materials, I learned a few basic techniques on encryption and thus discovered the "notion" of ciphering. That is, I quickly concluded that if language could be coded, it made perfect logical sense that it could also be decoded. Thus began my attempts—primarily as a fun pastime—at discovering techniques for decoding or "ciphering" language. In my nascent effort at ciphering language, I developed what amounted to an acrostic technique. During the early years in my work—using this acrostic technique—I discovered a cipher in Sigmund Freud's (1997) work on sexuality.[3] As a result, it was no great leap on my part to suspect and then to look for a similar occurrence in Einstein's work once the "hook" had grabbed my attention.

I will have more to say about some of Freud's other work later, but in the interim, let me continue by pointing out what stood out like a sore thumb for me in the above quote. What hooked me was Einstein's usage of the term "fairest." Immediately upon reading the statement—and for some reason which I cannot adequately explain—I began to puzzle over what he might really have meant by the expression "fairest." I "eventually" reached the conclusion that he meant exactly what he said. When I say eventually, I mean I arrived at a conclusion with respect to this issue only after some exhaustive reading of most of the available writings attributed to Einstein's own hand. That is, I came to understand that he uses the term "fair" in the everyday conventional sense of the word. What he was obviously hinting is, in regard to the many things one could experience in one's lifetime, being exposed to and learning about the mysteries in life would afford one the best

4

opportunity to experience the highest quality of the life as we know it. That is, presumably, anyone in the possession of the additional facts of life as revealed in the mysteries would have the greater amount of information for the purposes of handling the exigencies or affairs of life. Consequently, having satisfied myself that I understood the sense in which Einstein used the expression "fairest," my thoughts immediately turned to the opposite scenario where one would not have been exposed to the "mysterious"—in the course of one's lifetime—as that which portends one having a less-fortunate life experience. At this point, the question for me became, what is the "mysterious" which Einstein mentioned? It appears he was using the word in a general sense. Within that context, the most immediate mystery for me was his theory of relativity. Reading his theory and related material, albeit interesting, is not bedtime literature. So in order to get a better understanding of what he was saying, I had to review some of the background information on his work. I ended up uncovering valuable tidbits, such as why he had to use Lorentz's equations in order to make his theoretical arguments work mathematically (Bohm, 1996). Eventually, I honed in on the pertinent substance by focusing on his equation $E = MC^2$.

As I began looking for the potential "mysterious" elements in the equation, I challenged myself to determine if some hidden puzzle was there waiting to be uncovered. Some years earlier, I had stumbled on a book on cryptography which made plain the existence of coding processes which made use of the letters of the alphabet. As a result of those readings, I suspected that there might be some meaning hidden in the letters of the equation. I did not retain a reference for my original source, but nevertheless, a recent book by Martin Gardner (1972), *Codes, Ciphers and Secret Writing*, is similar in content to the one I am referencing. That is, it too is a book about techniques for *sending* coded messages using numerical and letter codes. Nonetheless, what I am coaxing the reader to discover has not so much to do with the art of sending coded messages; rather, it has everything to do with being able to discern the code which is *already* embedded in the lexicon of language. Additionally, my training in mathematics had informed me of the utility of sometimes exploring for a method of proof of a theorem by considering the end of the proof first, what is to be proved, and then following the appropriate logical steps backwards toward the proof's beginning. As a result of this experience, I was intellectually comfortable and confident in concluding Einstein's equation was ripe for exploration. Moreover, in the above quote, Einstein himself suggested the mysterious "are only accessible to our reason in their most elementary forms." Of course, as a result of the exploratory readings I mentioned earlier, I was made aware of the one literary formulation of the equation which stated: "Energy is equal to mass times the speed of light squared" (Einstein, 2001, and Bodanis, 2000). I understood this to be a statement in physics, therefore one aspect of the mystery no longer existed for me with regard to what was represented to the public as the formal literary expression of the equation. Consequently, there only remained the elemental "form" of the equation, and to determine whether or not there might be a dual informal meaning hidden there; in other words, a possible double entendre. Scientific and mathematical equations typically use letters that are suggestive of the elemental facts under discussion. In the equation $E = MC^2$, the E suggests the word "energy," the letter M suggests the word "mass," but the letter C is not suggestive of the word "light." However, light does in fact help us to "see," so in that sense, the word "light" might be suggestive of the letter C [see].

I puzzled over the form of this equation for a non-specific period, until, in an epiphany, I finally saw what the *interpretive* hidden mystery was. Of course, one must recognize an epiphany is not born in a vacuum. Years of study, through the readings of a plethora of diverse materials, sundry life experiences, and a deliberate systematic use of my *imagination*—within an intellectual context—to develop the "presuppositions" (Hegel, 1969)—or domain assumptions if you will—

essential to insight, all contributed to my being privileged to experience the revelation. Not surprisingly then, I knew on first glance it was a significant discovery. I had discovered the second half of what minimally was a duality in the literary formulation of meanings in the equation. Of course, there certainly remains the possibility of additional levels of meaning being present there, so I want to be careful not to imply that one is limited to just two layers of meaning. However, it shall definitely become clear that minimally the two meanings I am discussing—the initial one given and secondarily, the one I discovered—do in fact exist. As a consequence, what was once opaque to me suddenly became at least translucent. The insight occurred to me roughly in the following proximate piecemeal fashion:

$$E = MC^2$$
E = M times C squared
HE = M TIMES C SQUARED
HE = HIM C'S SQUARE
HE = MAN C'S SQUARED
HE (generic he) = MAN (generic man) SEES SQUARE

My explorations, together with at least one of the presuppositions I had previously made about the origin of language and its symbolic structures, enabled me to settle on the final generic version above as the secondary meaning in the elementary form of Einstein's equation.[4] That is, the version which states: HE = MAN SEES SQUARE. The reason I evolved the word "he" from the letter "e," and the "him" from the letter "m" is because they rhymed phonetically and it made sense with respect to my original presuppositions. The process is analogous to what Hegel would call a "Notion of the Notion" (ibid., p. 582).[5]

You can readily appreciate the second interpretive meaning of Einstein's equation by focusing on the term "square" in the expression. The average modern dictionary will affirm the term "square" in slang means conventional or conservative in style or outlook; and more pointedly, it refers to a person who is *not hip* to what is really going on in his/her immediate environment or in the world. The expression "square" then has a pejorative connotation. Consequently, I concluded some positive and constructively assertive "action" or response was being proposed, and was to be initiated on the part of the so-called "man" in this relation upon being made aware of or discovering the existence of an individual characterized as being a "square." The notion appears as a relation between an adult and a child, and one where the adult needs to educate and guide the child into adulthood. The equilibrium in the equation is facilitated by the independent element "square" being acted upon by the "man sees." It appears as though the so-called square is to be subjected to a training procedure, whose outcome is to be the creation of the dependent "he," in this sense, a matured and acutely aware adult. That is, as a square one would undergo a very subtle and intellectually sophisticated form of hazing designed to inform their adulthood. It then follows the word "heart" refers to the "art" of creating a "he" where the generic "man" would be the catalytic agent. Early on, this sense of the term "heart" came to mind when I reflected on Sigmund Freud's reported use of the term "dis-ease" as meaning "disease" or uneasiness; a fact which David Matza (1969) recorded in a footnote (ibid. p. 49). Rendering a word in its syllabication can expand its meaning. That is, the word "heart" is readily partitioned into "he-art," and its meaning in this form, as explained above, is larger than the conventional meaning and far from trivial. (For as he thinketh in his heart, so is he . . . [Pro. 23:7]).

The remainder of this book will be devoted to all those who doubt the validity and merit of what I am acknowledging and giving expression to above. It is not my intention to get into the details of just how a particular individual is transformed into the *kind* of mature adult suggested above. That process is sufficiently explained by David Matza (ibid.) in his book *Becoming Deviant*. I choose instead to reveal the significance of these findings and explain what the results mean for people in general now that some of the results of the process stand discovered and ready to be revealed. There is something surprising and even ironic about the results of the aforementioned actions. The point where one purportedly ends up in the maturation process—mentally possessing a sense of being aware—is only the very *beginning* of the true learning experience I am referencing in this book. Learning really begins only after the individual can be made to see beyond the veil of his or her previously taken-for-granted ways of thinking. The neophyte cannot even begin to imagine the vastness of the subtleties of knowledge, which lie beyond our conventional ways of understanding our symbolic universe. Growing that level of learning will necessarily have to be done at the reader's leisure and over the course of a lifetime. My goal is to demonstrate to the reader how the simple *anagram*—as a form of an example—is a very efficient tool with which to accomplish the effort.[6] Any modern dictionary will explain an anagram as being the creation of a new word or phrase from a given word or phrase, by simply commuting or transposing the letters in the original word or phrase. I will have more to say about anagrams in a latter chapter. In the meantime, I can inform the patient reader that the journey of this book represents the experience of descending out of the clouds of conventional wisdom and finding the meaning and usage of the word "heart" within a relevant context. Within that context, the word "heart" refers to the art and practice of cleverly causing or promoting adult maturation on an intellectual and practical level. Additionally, the reader will come to recognize that my present exposition is a touchdown on the "*anagrammatic*" earth the device will help you to discover and enable you to use. For example, if the first letter "h" of the word "heart" is made to be the last letter in the word, we evolve the word "earth." Similarly, a rearrangement or commutation of the letters in the word "wolf" can yield the word "flow." Thus we quickly discover an anagram is a useful tool for re-exploring potential word and even sentence content.

For me the mystery contained in the above equation had suddenly run the gamut from an opaque unknown, through something translucent and vague, and finally to a patent transparency. This was especially evident once I located its overall significance within the context of what I had learned over the years under the rubric of the "Sociology of Knowledge" (Mannheim, 1936, and Merton, 1957). The sociology of knowledge refers to the study and sociological analysis of everything that mankind passes off as acquired knowledge and the ways in which that knowledge is shaped by social factors. Furthermore, it should be noted that the meaning we just developed from the elemental form of Einstein's most famous equation is an example of the kind of thing he is referencing, when he speaks of the "manifestations of the profoundest reason," in portions which are "never so [too] tiny." One can theoretically reach levels of understanding where even individual letters reveal a content equivalent to whole words and complete thoughts—if not sentences. With this information in hand as my foundation, I began forging an expanded key. This is the real significance of Einstein's equation for me. The equation provided me with the first few letters of a key. By this I mean I began experimenting with and subsequently creating word and letter keys centered around our standard twenty-six-letter alphabet, which conformed to my own presuppositions about the origin of language and its presumed content. Moreover, this creative process was the natural response to what I had before me as a student of knowledge. Hegel gives a full expression to what is to be understood here when he states:

> Hence there is for it [the elementary universal—in this case Einstein's equation $E = MC^2$] a higher universal, and for this again a higher, and so on, in the first instance, to infinity. For cognition [the ability to think] here considered there is no immanent limit, since it starts from the given, and the form of abstract universality [construction on the basis of letters like in the equation itself] is characteristic

10

of its prius [original form]. Therefore any subject matter whatever that seems to possess an elementary universality is made the subject matter of a specific science, and is an absolute beginning to the extent that ordinary thought is presupposed to be acquainted with it and it is taken on its own account as requiring no derivation. Definition takes it as immediate (ibid., p. 803).

The above quote by Hegel gives credence to a pivotal idea or notion. That is, if you begin a theory with a particular set of basic elements, any science founded on those elements will have been constructed using those same basic elements. Since I started my definition of Einstein's equation on the basis of what I perceived from the *letters* in his equation, it makes sense that what would evolve in terms of the "new thought" would be a science of a type based on letters. Thus the anagrams I will develop are actually the mini-proofs of the new system. In chapter 4, I will share a collection of examples of anagrams, using a neutral key I developed from the aforementioned experimentation. I label it a "neutral" key because it permits us to learn, yet all the while remain at a reasonably safe distance from some of the politically sensitive topics, which I discovered other keys of this type could reveal.

At this point, I need to clarify some anticipated questions and issues lest the reader run off under the false impression that what was just revealed was easy to discover and explain. It was not! One obvious question is whether or not my revelations on contents of this nature will—with respect to this level of knowledge—be exhaustive? Let me proclaim unequivocally, despite the depth and breadth of the knowledge which will issue from it, the present exposition does not even come close to registering a significant measure on any scale of material facts which may be considered to be exhaustive. The present exposition is intended merely to make plain the existence of a public-key-cipher in language in general, and to interpret certain segments of it. It is not intended to give an exhaustive or even a definitive exposition of these matters. Since language is by nature open-ended, and ciphers are inherently malleable, an exhaustive or definitive account of these subjects is a virtual impossibility. However, all encrypted or coded materials are vulnerable to ciphers: that is, they are vulnerable first to being discovered and then to their being systematically unraveled or reduced, if you will. The codes mentioned do appear to have been predetermined and to permeate all language, and are so refined they have both literary and numerical elements. This fact becomes particularly evident when one uses techniques of the kind being discussed to analyze so-called "rigorous" scientific materials.

The craft of directly and proficiently *writing* a public-key-cipher appears to be a special and formidable skill which would necessarily require a *prior* knowledge of the proscribed standardized key or keys in use, along with some knowledge of the societal or overall linguistic master plan. Moreover, one would additionally need to have the ability to write a greatly reduced abstract of any given text, which is desired to be *hidden*; thus, capturing the desired main thoughts while remaining true to and utilizing the given key. These keys are in the possession of certain "privileged" elements in our society. By privileged I do not mean privileged merely in the conventional sense of having inherited or been handed the information and skill; albeit, it is obvious, there are many who are conveniently given systematic formal training in these matters. On the contrary, I mean privileged to have acquired the understanding at all, regardless of their status in life or the means by which they acquired it. It is my hope that without too much effort, the reader of my book will in time discover and learn to appreciate that all of this knowledge is readily available to and, more profoundly, already in the possession of the man on the street, despite its academic and intellectual trappings. Moreover, having obviously gone through numerous refinements, the general key structure is millennial in age and origin. In fact, I am firmly convinced the seeds of the structure of language speak to the actual "method," in regard to the origin and the underpinnings of the concept of language itself. In my effort to facilitate the discussion of these matters, the reader would benefit from my eliciting the help of Sigmund Freud in clarifying some crucial modern and relevant concepts.

Initially, I want to make the trivial observation that most of the pivotal concepts used by both Einstein and Freud predate them just as most living ideas predate each of us. For example, Freud's most seminal work was on the interpretation of dreams. The fact that man has practiced interpreting dreams, even in antiquity, can be made witnessed to in the extended discussion of dream interpretation occurring in the second chapter of the book of Daniel in the Holy Bible. This fact notwithstanding, Sigmund Freud's (1952) important ancillary contribution to our understanding in general comes from his use of the concepts of "manifest" and "latent" content, which we need to borrow from his dream interpretation theory. In describing his approach and technique of dream interpretation, Freud states that:

> In order to contrast the dream as it is retained in my memory with the relevant material discovered by analyzing it, I will speak of the former as the "manifest content of the dream" and the latter—without, in the first instance, making any further distinction—as the "latent content of the dream" (ibid., p. 16).

He further clarifies and expands the meanings he intends here when he states:

> I shall describe the process, which transforms the latent into the manifest content of dreams as the "dream work." The counterpart to this activity—one which brings about a transformation in the opposite direction—is already

known to us as the work of analysis (ibid.).[7]

This nonchalant and seemingly non-extrusive comment is much more profound than it might initially appear. His definition here of "dream work" is consistent with what had been discussed earlier, about one having the ability to write a public-key-cipher. That is, the latent content of this material can be known, because once written down the manifest content will be found to have been created from what will be exposed as its latent content, and of course, the rediscovered latent content will itself have meaning. The above facts additionally suggest that a dream is a phenomenon born from an individual's real-time exposure to a specific symbolic and linguistic content. The reader has to come to understand that "nothing just happens." The "profundity" in the reasoning here is that we come to know things because they were already known.[8]

The initial manifest content then would be comprised of all of what was remembered from the actual dream. The latent content would come from an analysis of the formal, "written" recording of the manifest dream content. Thus an analysis of the original manifest content represents a cipher of the original manifest content revealing a "secondary" manifest content or "latent" content. This latent content is revealed and necessarily interpreted by a particular cipher, a special key or interpretive device. These devices and related techniques may or may not be what is contained in advanced versions of conventional "content analysis" (Holsti, 1969). Thus the latent content becomes the relevant material for the appropriate analysis and resultant dream interpretation. Additionally, Freud appears here to categorize the interpretation of the original manifest content without the use of a cipher, but rather, by the mere use of conventional word meanings as simply "analysis."

No matter, what I wish for the reader to understand is not Freud's use of the concepts of manifest and latent content within the context of dream interpretation, but rather, their use in a general way, and in relation to what I am discussing in this book. The two concepts are sound and thus will be useful to us within the present work. For example, when I discussed the primary (MANIFEST) meaning of the elemental form of Einstein's equation above ($E = MC^2$), we got "energy is equal to mass times the speed of light squared." However, an analysis of the equation within a larger theoretical framework yielded a revealing secondary (LATENT) meaning, "he is equal to man sees square." It is significant that appropriate theoretical frameworks assist us in seeing behind the veil or, rather, assist us in seeing into the complex. The current usage of the concepts of manifest and latent content, as they may be applied to any written materials, will be essential to our understanding of what follows. Additionally, it is important to emphasize that it appears possible to cipher a latent content for any symbolic material that can be translated into a standard language. Moreover, having the ability to discern the latent content of any substantive material in no way diminishes the primary meaning or face value of that material, its manifest content. Using the terminology of Michael Polanyi (1958), the idea of manifest content is consistent with "the articulate contents of science," and latent content with what he refers to as "the unspecifiable art of scientific research" (ibid., p. 53). It is "unspecifiable" primarily because the process is difficult to put into words. In this regard, it is clear the manifest content defines the objective reality, while latent content is a reflection of the fact that a subjective reality exists and is also to be brought into consideration (Berger and Luckmann, 1966).

It is instructive to highlight another writer who has used Freud's terminology of manifest and latent content. I had not read his book in over twenty-five years, yet it was very comforting to have "rediscovered"—if you will—the renowned sociologist Robert K. Merton (1957) who has also "adapted" the concept of manifest and latent meanings from Freud. Merton uses these Freudian constructions in his theory of functionalism, which is outlined in his seminal work *Social Theory and Social Structure* (ibid., p. 61). In that work, he specifies at least four distinct "heuristic purposes" (ibid., p. 64) for using Freud's concepts. Moreover, the four purposes outlined by Merton, point to why Freud's concepts are so apropos to the present book. That is, the four purposes which Freud's comments awakened in Merton also helps bring a more acute vision to the purpose of my book. Having read Merton's work years earlier probably helped me as well. I personally think it somehow not coincidental that the four purposes outlined by Merton, on nearly a line-item basis, reflects the very method of my current book.[9] However, I have neither deliberately nor consciously followed Merton's formulations on these matters. The spontaneous occurrence of my work, to some extent, mirroring portions of Merton's work obviously exemplifies just how much our thought processes are influenced by what we read. Especially when by direct experience, what we have read becomes truly meaningful in our everyday lives. Basically, the reason why both Merton and I have chosen Freud's language is because it, as Merton states it, has a "heuristic purpose" in that it "clarifies the analysis" (ibid.) of substantive materials within relative contexts. Most importantly, Merton very efficiently explains the relative value of latent content over and above. or in contrast to, that of the manifest content of material information. In building on a concept which had its earlier revelation in the sociology of Max Weber (Weber, 1958, and Peter Berger, 1963, p. 38), Merton points out the *latent* content always represents the "unconscious," the "unintended and unrecognized" (Merton, 1957, p. 63) elements in substantive materials. He further states this "not common knowledge," which is principally found in the latent aspects of material facts, "represent a greater increment in knowledge than findings involving manifest" (ibid., p. 68) material content. That is, and this is an invaluable point, one simply can learn more through the study of the latent revelations of material facts than they can through the manifest revelations.

Lastly, like Merton, I too have independently discovered that latent contents typically "run counter to prevailing moral evaluations" (ibid., p. 71), and "*opinionated attitudes*," if you will. On this most essential point, when referencing Freud's opinion on the subject, Philip Rieff (1959) states that: "True self-awareness is impossible until the moralizing voice is restrained, or at least controlled" (ibid., p. 78). This theory too is among the more important concepts mentioned in this book. To get inside of what is being discussed here, the reader must *allow* his/her self-awareness to be extended and broadened. The reader cannot fully appreciate the levels of knowledge and understanding I am describing if he/she continues to maintain a *moralizing posture* and interject what most often is his/her own narrow opinion on what is being discussed. Holier-than-thou attitudes and opinions do not allow the reader to possess the level of sensitivity needed to penetrate to an understanding of the matters currently before us. What one needs to adopt is an *attitude* of study possessed by those of us who are not concerned to stand in moral judgement over what we discover during our research. In contrast, we are those who are thoroughly intent on simply completely understanding and accepting what we discover in the things we choose to research. In order to appreciate the deeper meanings in these matters one has to "suspend" (Matza, 1969, p. 137) one's taken-for-granted opinions and convenient disbelief. Although Merton is using these concepts within a different context than I am, I would urge every reader of my book to review, first-hand, Merton's original general comments on the above topics (Merton, 1957, pp. 60–84).

Moreover, although the apparatus exists for the analysis of the manifest content of dreams, a case might be made for never voluntarily subjecting one's dreams to public scrutiny much less deliberate interpretation. I believe our dream lives are, for the most part, inherently intended merely to be experienced. In regard to these matters, an argument could be made to the effect that the very nature of a public analysis of the dream would yield a potential alteration, a qualitative if not also a quantitative change, in the structure of the analyzed item, therefore an alteration in substance. To alter the substance is to change its interpretation, thus changing its meaning and use. This change is a result of the relation existent within and the force occurring within—what Einstein (1983) reminds us is—the "ether." I will limit my comments here about the "ether" because a discussion of the "ether" is beyond the intended and specific scope of the present book and is not for the uninitiated. Within this context, however, the "ether" concerns our relationship to everyone and everything else on the planet. It implies, willy-nilly, that we all live together on this planet submerged inside a symbolic universe of discourse, from which we cannot escape and which affects our everyday lives. Regardless, as Freud (1952) relates it to us:

> Popular opinion . . . seems to persist in the belief that .
> . . dreams have a meaning, which relates to the prediction
> of the future and which can be discovered by some process
> of interpretation of a content which is often confused and
> puzzling (ibid., p. 7).

Despite my own reservations on the matter of dream interpretation, let me suggest we be careful not to take for granted and casually dismiss what Freud is saying here about "popular" wisdom on the issue of interpretation of things in general. With respect to dreams, he is saying the "popular opinion" of the man on the street would have us understand the skill of dream interpretation is for the specific purpose of predicting the future. The notion that the content of a dream can be used to predict the future—if true, and even if he merely means having the ability to make a definitive "statement" of insight into the future—is not a trivial comment to be glossed over. However, I am not interested in what Freud is revealing about the "popular opinion" on dream interpretation, but rather, I am impressed and comforted by the extent to which Freud values popular opinion. For shortly after making the above observation, Freud makes the following definitive statement regarding popular opinion. He states:

> One day I discovered to my great astonishment that the view of dreams, which came nearest to the truth, was not the medical [formal professional] but the popular one, half- involved though it still was in superstition (ibid., p. 8).

Before continuing, several additional points should be made about the significance of the notions of manifest and latent content. The first point is that all the forms of literature and communication that we come into contact with being worldly entities possess a manifest and a latent content. Separately, the manifest and latent forms are replete with varying meanings and content. Their actual contents then are to an extent essentially unrelated. That is, the notions of manifest and latent content underscores the fact minimally, it appears, a deliberate humanly engineered or socially constructed dualism exists within the very structure of all formal and conventional human knowledge and communication, as we know it. Some might argue the latent aspects of this duality are a completely "unintended, unforeseen," or "unrecognized" consequence of the empirical structure of language in general. I would suggest this is only a half-truth. As a matter of fact, I have found that language is, more often than not, keyed toward a well-defined latent content. In this regard, conventional wisdom refers to the everyday manifest content of the given knowledge. The discovery of the mysteries then refers both to an individual's initial realization of the fact that a latent content actually exists everywhere, and also to the potentially limitless body of atypical yet meaningful information to be uncovered by reviewing the latent content once it is revealed. It should not be overlooked; in fact, the point should be made, that even Freud (ibid.) himself was aware of the significance of his applications of the concepts of manifest and latent content. According to Freud:

> The transformation of the latent dream thoughts into

the manifest dream content deserves all our attention, since it is the first instance known to us of psychical material being changed over from one mode of expression to another, from a mode of expression, which is immediately intelligible to us to another which we can only come to understand with the help of guidance and effort, though it, too, must be recognized as a function of our mental activity (ibid., p. 18).

The above quote refers again, most specifically, to what Freud called the "dream work" which is the skill of transforming latent content into manifest content. Here, he emphasizes that the technique "deserves all our attention." As a matter of fact, and it is in no way coincidental, the *primary* goal of my book is to help turn the reader's attention in that very direction. At its core, my book is concerned with the nature of mental activity of the above type, and how certain well-defined mental activities can help to inform us within our everyday world. One such mental activity is referred to as "sensibility" (Kant, 1965). Through subsequent discussions, the reader will come to understand that the contextual meaning of "sensibility" is actually "sense ability." It is the heightened or enhanced ability to "sense" things previously taken for granted or not previously noticed in our immediate mental and physical environment. If I am allowed to paraphrase Freud (ibid.) by adding my emphasis to his comments, we can observe Freud coming very close to describing the real-time practical technique used to help develop one's "sensibility." While discussing a proposed "technique" for "the solution of phobias, obsessions, and delusions, etc." (ibid., p. 8), Freud stated:

The discovery of the trains of thought which, [initially] concealed from consciousness, connect the [problematic] . . . idea with the remaining contents of the mind is equivalent to a resolution of the symptoms [experiencing problematic thoughts] and has as its consequence the mastering [controlling] of [these] ideas which till then could not be inhibited . . . this procedure is easily described, although instruction and practice would be necessary before it could be put into effect if we [were to] make use of it [the technique or practice of utilizing the problematic idea] on someone else, let us say . . . we [would] require him to direct his attention on to the idea in question, not, however, to reflect upon it as he has done so often already, but to take notice of whatever occurs to his mind without any exception and report it [write it down] (ibid., pp. 8–9).

Taking the time to literally *write* down on paper and study what the sensed mental images are, is pivotal to one's capturing and appreciating how focusing on objects our senses *direct* us to can efficiently assist in raising our levels of consciousness. Not to mention, this simple habit will deliver into our hands unexpected facts to be perceived. ("Of these things put them in remembrance, charging them before the Lord that they strive not about words to no profit, but to the subverting of the hearers [those with sensibility on the psychical or extrasensory levels]. Study to show thyself approved unto God, a workman that needeth not to be ashamed, rightly dividing the word of truth" [2 Tim. 2:14–15]).[10] Freud is clearly of the opinion that something can potentially be done to further the individual subject's personal development on the matter of sensibility:

If we can induce him to abandon his criticism of the ideas that occur to him, and to continue pursuing the trains of thought which will emerge so long as he keeps his attention turned upon them [the ideas and even the actual words that define the ideas], we find ourselves in possession of a quantity of psychical [literary, spiritual, and phonetically aided] material, which we soon find is clearly connected with the . . . [problematic] idea which was our starting point; this material will soon reveal connections between the . . . [problematic] idea and other ideas, and will eventually enable us to replace the [problematic] idea by a new one which fits into the nexus of thought in an intelligible fashion it will therefore be enough to say that we obtain material that enables us to resolve any . . . [problematic] idea if we turn our attention precisely to those associations which are "involuntary," which "interfere with our reflection," and which are normally dismissed by our critical faculty as worthless rubbish (ibid., pp. 9–10).

The importance and the power of the discussion developed above represents just how close Freud has come in this excerpt to describing what the "ostensible"[11] writer Immanuel Kant refers to as "sensibility"— and that which others have referred to as *getting in touch with the Holy Spirit.*[12] By using the technique of writing things down, we eventually acquire the ability to "obtain material" useful to our understanding, which we once considered to be "worthless rubbish." For example, there are times when some of the individual words seem to jump off the pages while reading. Whether we are conscious of it or not, those words inform ruminations, and we often find our thoughts drifting away from the written materials. What Freud is telling us is, if we write those words down as they occur, in the end we discover a meaningful and useful content in those words, and in the interim, we are able to remain focused on what we are presently doing. Additionally, if one would continue in this practice, one would develop the awareness to notice other important cues in one's immediate environment. At some point, I will have more to say about this matter of sensibility.

Of course the reader will need me to expand upon what is being discussed in this chapter in order to put the major interpretations and their significance in perspective. To completely accomplish the task, I will be obliged in a later chapter to present you with some appropriate characteristic examples. First, however, I must continue by taking the time to escort the reader through some informal yet related discussion, in my effort to lay the appropriate groundwork for the examples.

ENDNOTES

1 One should be careful not to immaturely jump to the conclusion, Einstein did not believe in God. Such a conclusion would be taking the present quote out of context. However, any definitive discussion about the character of Einstein's faith is beyond the scope of this book.

2 My definition and use of the term "cipher" is consistent with any good dictionary's various contextual meanings. That is, a good dictionary will define all the contextual senses in which I use this singular term.

3 The discussion involved concern over sexual permissiveness among youth and homosexuals, and the possible societal remedies for the behavior, which included a debate over the possible deliberate introduction of sexual transmitted diseases into those populations.

4 The word "generic" means the general sense in which the word "he" could just as easily be replaced by the word "she," etc.

5 You should appreciate that the idea of a "notion" here means, in the informal conventional sense, you're just having a vague image or sense of something. To reach the relevant notion, it was necessary for me to make use of some presuppositions. The one presupposition I specifically applied here is that all language and symbolic forms are permeated with sexual connotations. I had based this particular

presupposition on some others that I had made about the origin of language in general. In regard to the other presuppositions, I have chosen to exercise my prerogative not to discuss the majority of them. For the most part, I consider the specific presuppositions privileged information. Moreover, the fact that I would not share all of my own presuppositions with a general public will not be too troubling to you, once you begin to appreciate the extent to which the one I just shared with you is significant. Besides, presuppositions as statements are not necessarily implied fact. Their only original authority is their usefulness toward assisting in a process of exploration. Furthermore, it is important, with specific regard to presuppositions, I not taint your view with my version of the so-called "facts." The larger secrets must be discovered on their own terms to maintain their integrity. To this end, you will not benefit from blindly holding on to my coat tails. This book is keyed to a delimited set of domain assumptions of the above type. The reason for this will become clear during the remainder of the text.

[6]   The reader should rely on any modern dictionary definition of the term, for this initial meaning of anagram. I will make additional comments regarding my own use of the concept of anagram during the course of the text, and will finish explaining my interpretation and use of the concept in chapter four, where numerous examples of my style of anagrams will also be supplied.

[7]   I believe what Freud means by "analysis" is consistent with one of the senses in which I use the term cipher. That is, the application or use of special techniques to analyze written material, and which give us access to the material's secret latent content. This is to be contrasted with the contemporary technique of "content analysis." See the Ole R. Holsti reference on "content analysis."

⁸   In view of these revelations, Freud's major book on *The Interpretation of Dreams* (1965) now potentially appears to be a much more profound work than I initially would have imagined. Any review of that work using the technique that I am currently discussing would be a special and separate project from the present one.

⁹   Merton (ibid., pp. 64–82) outlines the following "heuristic" results of latent content analysis:

a. "Clarifies the analysis of seemingly irrational social patterns."
b. "Directs attention to theoretically fruitful fields of inquiry."
c. "The discovery . . . represents significant increments in sociological knowledge."
d. "Precludes the substitution of naïve moral judgements for sociological analysis."

¹⁰   In addition to serving Merton's purposes, the above points represent the major implications, purpose, and method of my present book.

¹¹   I sometimes use the word "ostensible" when referring to authors. I do this as a result of my discovery that the cipher of an author's name often has a direct meaning in relation to the actual discussion in progress. It leads me to believe that what we are perhaps often dealing with, with regard to some purported historical figures, are actually pseudonyms for individuals and/or groups, and not necessarily the given names of real persons. The name Immanuel Kant is a perfect example of what I mean. Example of the following anagrams:

Immanuel Kant

I'm [I am]	I'm [I am]
Manual	Manual
N [in]	T [teach]

T [time]	E [me]
E [we]	N [in]
K [ok];	K [ok],etc.

12   I have embedded Bible verses in the text where apropos. My reason for doing so is to help the reader appreciate that Bible verse is relevant to the everyday issues of life, and ultimately, to demonstrate that Bible verse plays an integral role in this discussion.

The contextual relevance of these anagrams becomes apparent as one continues by including anagrams composed from the title and other content of Kant's book, *Critique of Pure Reason*, whose detail I need not delve into at the moment. In fact, as a result of my cursory review of the matter, I am now inclined to believe that author's names sometimes do not represent individuals at all; rather, the names are *surreptitious* pseudonyms representing some material content, and/or are symbolic of a group of individuals. Of course, any of the above insight on the anagrammatic content of names can be applied to names in general.

Chapter Two

I Think You Need to Know!

Amazing grace—how sweet the sound—that saved a wretch like me! I once was lost but now am found, was blind but now I see.
—Newton, 1977, Hymn # 132

There are many reasons why people write books. I wrote this book because I believe anyone with the ability to read deserves the "fairest" chance to have the best human life experience possible. More importantly, because the path to the level of knowledge and understanding being explored here is so convoluted, I finally felt compelled to write it down in a coherent form, and to leave it as my primary contribution to mankind's living history.

The present book has turned out to be part of a book I considered writing fifteen years ago, but at that time, I was tentative and even thought that I would never write the book or anything even remotely related to it. At the time, I knew I did not have enough of a command of the subject to write about it, that is, enough of a command of the major critical issues to safely share the ideas with others. In fact, even now, I consider this book to have written itself, and I have only been a conduit through which it is being presented. ("Then I said, I will not make mention of him, nor speak anymore in his name, but his work was in mine heart as a fire shut up in my bones, and I was weary with forbearing and I could not stay [remain silent]" [Jer 20: 9].) One should understand that books are to be mastered in all their inner workings.

28

They are tools, and should be treated as such. Thus, the present book is a refinement of a potentially larger one considered earlier and is, in its present form by design, a mechanism or device for counteracting what I refer to as generational curses. I define a "generational curse" to be any deliberate action or inaction that negatively affects a person or group, carrying itself over from one generation of individuals to the next, and preventing or limiting one's ability to be the best one can be in society. It represents a set of circumstances and perspectives that prevent individuals from having a fair opportunity to experience the highest possible quality of life. That is, generational curses are obstacles to productive everyday living, which either unnecessarily delay or prevent individuals from being his/her best, emotionally and intellectually, and thus able to share in the better opportunities of life. For example, those actions, which historically can be considered racial, ethnic, or gender discriminatory practices fall within the category of a generational curse.

To be the victim of a generational curse is like being confined in a social and intellectual box. One's intellectual, artistic, and technical vision along with other social opportunities are unnecessarily limited in every instance where a generational curse is being manifested. Consequently, when one is young, innocent, and impressionable, being socialized in such a negative way can result in one wasting most of one's lifetime attempting to rectify the inherent negative effects of the unfairness of a generational curse. If we consider the infinity of knowledge and the quality of understanding potentially available to us, why should the majority of every new generation of persons born on earth be relegated to starting from the bottom? Like all other generations before them, their effort is to achieve relative parity in understanding the best ways to think and behave in society and everyday life. In my opinion, given the existing conventional ways of viewing our social world, by the time an individual is situated to understand enough and begin positively building toward having a good life, many essentially needless mistakes will have been made. One will then necessarily have to endure a transitional period in one's life, of correcting for the mistakes, before real progress can truly begin and he/she is able to find his/her social compass in life. Let no one be deceived, our lives are finite and this needless time wasting during our lives is, in my opinion, the most heinous by-product of a generational curse. Thus misinformation and insufficient information, in one's youth, with respect to the basic facts and perspectives for successful living is a generational curse. Of course, there are those who would consider thinking in the above critical manner "dangerous thought." In fact, as one very influential scholar, Karl Mannheim (1936), informs us:

> That there is an area of "dangerous thought" in every society is scarcely debatable. While we recognize that what is dangerous to think about may differ from country to country and from epoch to epoch, on the whole the subjects marked with the danger signal are those which the society or the controlling elements in it believe to be so vital and hence so sacred that they will not tolerate their profanation by discussion. But what is not so easily recognized is the fact that thought, even in the absence of official censorship, is disturbing, and, under certain conditions, dangerous and subversive. For thought is a catalytic agent that is capable of unsettling routines, disorganizing habits, breaking up customs, undermining faiths, and generating skepticism.

He goes on to say:

> The distinctive character of social science discourse is to be sought in the fact that every assertion, no matter how objective it may be, has ramifications extending beyond the limits of science itself. Since every assertion of a "fact" about the social world touches the interests of some individual

or group, one cannot even call attention to the existence of certain "facts" without courting the objections of those whose very raison d'etre in society rests upon a divergent interpretation of the "factual" situation (ibid., pp. xiv–xv).

What is implied in Mannheim's comments is that "factual" information is sometimes deliberately distorted when its distortion is useful to the particular interests of certain individuals, groups, or societies. The fact that special interests often involve themselves in dirty tricks should not be news to anyone with minimal skills of observation and a decent attention span. What is significant to note is *how* "thought" can come to be considered "dangerous." Whenever thought is considered dangerous, it has *attained the value* of a "catalytic agent that is capable of unsettling routines." As a thing of *value*, the alleged dangerous thought cannot be devalued. It can never lose its intrinsic utility and power. Consequently, the way to neutralize the thought is to direct people away from the thought by deliberate misdirection or by scandalizing the thought. On the other hand, routine ways of thinking become imbedded in our memories and, as such, fade from our conscious focus becoming voluntary actions and related thoughts taken-for-granted. Poor habits of thought considered as thought taken-for-granted is what can be unsettled by atypical and critical thought. That is, poor habits of thought can be unsettled by the types of thought that challenge our routine wisdom. An example of a poor habit of thought, as thought taken-for-granted, is expressed in the concept of "solipsism." Solipsistic thought is a far too common form of poor thought where people believe that the physical brain, without the benefit of received information and knowledge, inherently contains all the knowledge an individual needs. Thus, in their tacit and naïve opinion, there is really no need for reading and studying to grow one's knowledge. Thoughts of the solipsistic type, as poor habits of mind and thought taken-for-granted, are a primary type of the substance in generational curses—that is, ignorance. Solipsist thought is prevalent among Black school kids who would criticize and make fun of their peers who attend school and actually take learning seriously. To the extent that this kind of negative peer group pressure is effective, it has the impact of draining the formal intellectual infrastructure of a social group and thereby negatively impacting the group as a whole with respect to socioeconomic standing. Ethnic youths who consistently have negative attitudes toward learning have been seriously miscued by the adult "significant others" in their culture with respect to the rules of the game in the "socialization process" (Hans Gerth and C. Wright Mills, 1964). These are the mental constructs of people who are content to be consumers only, and not producers of the capital goods in society. Consequently, it is obvious that large numbers of these so- called significant others have poor socialization skills themselves. They literally need to study or be taught what the *socialization process* really means. I say this because I have come to believe certain cultural attitudes are not accidents. They are born of common sentiments that quietly regenerate themselves and often have well-defined premises that support a particular societal outlook and lifestyle. Then again, just because one might come to disagree with some activity or behavior, however, does not automatically imply that there actually is something inherently wrong with it. There are reasons why individuals and groups of people consistently do what they do. Society and its reality are largely a deliberate "social construction" (Berger and Luckmann, 1966) and not an accidental occurrence, with arbitrary rules to be completely reinvented for each new generation of children. If a habit of mind is repeated from generation to generation, within a particular segment of society. there is a reason for its inveterate recurrence. Individuals and groups may use many forms of casuistry to justify why they do what they do. Practicing a generational curse might even be an unwitting behavior. These facts notwithstanding, group acceptance of a habit of mind does not disqualify it as representing a generational curse. On the contrary, group acceptance of what in effect amounts to a generational curse makes the issue all the more poignant.

The Mind Factory

I think most people would be surprised when they discover what types of knowledge, in the opinion of some elements in our society, qualify as dangerous thoughts. To begin with, there are certain ideas, which are essential to securing a true understanding of language and the meanings within language, for example, the concept of "taking-words-for-granted." The concept has been used formally to express the fact that the average person reads and rarely looks up words he/she does not know the meanings of, and rarely reviews words he/she claim to be familiar with (Hayakawa, 1941). Not establishing—and as needed, reviewing—the correct meanings of words as we learn to read would be all right I guess, if it were not for the fact that most people who practice these lazy habits never develop very marketable *formal skills*. Moreover, the lack of refinement in writing and verbal communication skills, on the part of those who practice these non-productive habits, will inevitably become very conspicuous. Witness, for example, the individual who one is likely to have encountered whose speech is very stilted. They want to appear to know lots of words, but they typically misuse many of them. Words are like anything else of *value*. If one is not willing either to do what it takes to learn words in general or to do what it takes to acquire the appropriate common aplomb associated with "ten-dollar" word usage and maintain the aplomb, he/she might as well leave well enough alone. The notion of an individual needing to possess an *attitude* in favor of valuing the mastery of the language should apply as well and equally to whether one typically uses a lot of professional jargon, colloquialisms, popular slang or even invectives—curse words. Since language is our principal mode of communicating when using language, one should use whichever of the above forms, or combination of the forms, one uses most and use that language form *well*. I am certainly not suggesting one should make a routine of using a lot of invectives. Yet at the very least, common sense would suggest one avoid trivializing any of the various forms of language. Otherwise, one serves the best in language's usage no good purpose, and one cheapens what the experience-forged words of language are designed to do. That is, to provide us with the conceptual machinery pertinent to our successfully making a way for ourselves in society in regard to both the emotional, practical, and the intellectual affairs of life. For those individual readers of this book who, while in the process of reading it are taking-the-words-for-granted, along with taking the endnotes and the references for granted, much of what I am hoping for you to accomplish in reading my book will be lost on you.

Another apparently sensitive concept is the understanding of word meanings as they appear "in context." That is, word meanings vary slightly as they are used over time in everyday language. The recurring variations in the meaning given individual words yield a fuller representation of their true meaning, and ultimately embody the formal meaning of the word (Ogden and Richards, 1923). Finding the variety of meanings of individual words "in context" is how dictionaries are assembled. ("In the mouth of two or three witnesses shall every word be established" [2 Cor 13:1].) Thus word meanings are formally based on actual recorded usage. It is significant to recall that writing and reading were established long before the modern dictionary. Once appreciated, the above two concepts taken together can truly make language come alive for the learner who routinely reads. That is, if youths can be encouraged to develop a sincere interest in reading while developing an appreciation for the above two concepts, the written word would come alive for them. Additionally, if these same youths can be encouraged to master basic arithmetic and develop a genuine understanding of "alphabetical" order—learning its major usage thus its real value—no area of formal learning or other modes of success will ever be *technically* beyond their reach. And all of this can begin with something which is so basic yet totally fundamental, that is, adults must read to young children in order for them to appreciate reading. Children have to be read to routinely and assisted in the comprehension of phonetics until they eventually adopt the vital habit of reading on their own. Reading to children is the essential element, the main ingredient. That is true because the substance and essentials of all we as human beings can ever know has already been set down within the Bible and other books of our world's libraries.

Moreover, modern-day youth are often not taught a healthy appreciation for the importance of the concept of "imitation" (Tarde, 1962) in their lives. They are not informed of the importance of sometimes simply mimicking what they observe others do. Instead, the youths of today are encouraged to believe that being like others, even in some important ways, is shameful and uncouth or something to run away from. It would be invaluable to the everyday lives and to the emotional growth of our young were they encouraged, earlier on, to understand that our society and culture has been passed down by means of imitation through generations. That is, by individuals building on thousands of years of refined traditions where traditions themselves are nothing more than a "habit" of mind, and actions or practices imitated from the activities and characters of others who have lived before us (Hans Gerth and C. W. Mills, 1964). Thus the young should be encouraged to become unashamed of mimicking the best qualities they see in others. This practice is essential to a refined character. I have long suspected the above few critical concepts as being among those considered dangerous because most people appear to only whisper them, and they are rarely if ever found together and succinctly in books. No matter, if they are considered dangerous thoughts, there is not much anyone can do about it. Individuals in society deserve, through understanding, to have a "fair" chance at opportunity. As citizens of the world, we all need to have these and other concepts essential to understanding thoroughly explained to us, and not have them be dangled over our heads as some intellectual gauntlet. Consequently, I do not consider the above thought to be dangerous, and the above thought represents only the essential elements of the level of knowledge the reader is being introduced to.

Even science and research can never know all of the right questions to ask, much less the answers to all the questions, in the vastness of the unknowns which forever lay before us in society. There is so much to be known, and so much to continue learning in an individual's life, it makes little sense in modern times to continue playing games with a person's intellectual and emotional growth. In this instance, by intellectual growth I am not strictly referring to formal education. I am referring to the substantive content of all of what one is being exposed to as knowledge. Changes in our educational posturing seems even the more urgent, once it is seen how the current limits and habits proscribed in formal education promote an ethnic bias. Smug insular attitudes have the effect of immediately alienating the underprivileged, and most educators who practice this tactic are not unaware of its subtle and invisible yet consistently effective debilitating impact. Large segments of certain ethnic groups are still so physically and emotionally oppressed, they have not come to appreciate, and believe, they have the same right to share in the power of knowledge, by way of its ownership and usage, as any other group. They commonly allow themselves to be intellectually intimidated. The mastery of sound intellect and marketable skills is hard work. Therefore, if one is willing to be disciplined and do the hard work required, it is yours. Unless one is born into wealth and privilege, there are no true shortcuts.

In my assault on generational curses, I am of course assuming that the average reader will benefit from formal social science discourse once it has been seated in everyday language. While much of the content of my exposition has its foundation in the most valid and fundamental elements of formal social theory, I am foregoing the typical formal jargon, as best I can, in an attempt to write in a style which even the uninitiated can understand. I am additionally using what one might refer to as a "scrambled eggs" approach to teaching. In my opinion, it is an effective way to quickly develop the depth of understanding and breadth of knowledge that my readers are, even if they are not immediately aware they are, encountering. Of course, pundits could quickly label my style eclectic. This work rightly falls under the branch of knowing called "the Sociology of Knowledge" which, as a sub discipline of sociology, has a very rich *formal* heritage. However, potential pundits would do well to choose a different tact as criticism, because I am not writing this book to have it be strictly discipline oriented. That could only be accomplished in a larger more formal work of the type that I alluded to earlier. My present effort is purely expository and intended to reach the widest of potential audiences. My book should be considered the result of ideas conceived within the essence of "sociology" and of "pragmatism," and it represents my interpretation of the sociological style and tradition that C. Wright Mills (Mills, 1966) modeled. Consequently, I am deliberately writing in a somewhat informal style. Besides, this style provides me with the privilege of not having to take sides and get involved in controversies over subtle and complex theoretical arguments among theorists. Nor am I obliged to have to uncover all of the refined historical underpinnings of what is being discussed. In fact, I am using an approach that enables me not to be obligated to look too critically into or even compare the works of other theorists. This semi-formal approach permits me to engage in an active discussion of the intellectual work of a limited number of theorists, while at the same time engage in a passive discussion of the work of numerous theorists. I take the liberty of doing this because I am not writing to social scientists as social scientists in the traditional sense, but rather, I am writing this book to everyday people, the everyday person on the street, so to speak.

However, despite the above disclaimers, I think it important the reader be made aware that my approach to these discussions exhibits, in its essentials, principles applied in logic and pure mathematics. As Alfred Tarski (1995) expresses it: "the principles with which we shall get acquainted serve the purpose of securing for the knowledge acquired in logic and mathematics the highest possible degree of clarity and certainty" (ibid., p. 117). Of course, the question remains as to what exactly are these principles that are being referenced. The one fundamental principle is that not all significant terms used in our discussion need be well-defined to have definitive meaning, and in addition, the validity of other given word meanings, ideas, concepts—and certain whole contents supplied in a given context—will be required to be accepted on faith. I will have more to say about the idea of "faith" in subsequent comments. For the time being, it is additionally important the reader understand that while I will be describing, explaining, and justifying certain things in the materials that follow, certain information will be yielded to him/her on the basis of mere "revelation." Some of the materials to be explored will come by way of my interpreting a cipher; therefore, at times I will simply relate the content to the reader, without revealing the ciphers' key and expect him/her, early on, to simply accept on faith that what I am saying is true. In the final analysis, one must permit oneself to be patient with me in regard to this particular issue. If the reader does so, he/she shall eventually not only gain an appreciation of the nature of faith and the central position faith holds in the matters before us, but additionally, he/she shall in time also be in a position to understand the cipher technique I am introducing. This tact is consistent with what typically has to take place in scientific discovery anyway. For as Tarski goes on to relate:

> A method of procedure would be ideal, if it permitted us to explain the meaning of every expression occurring . . . and to justify each of its assertions. It is easy to see that this ideal can never be realized. In fact, when one tries to explain the meaning of an expression, one uses, of necessity, other expressions; and in order to explain, in turn, the meaning of these expressions, without entering into a vicious circle, one has to resort to further expressions again, and so on. We thus have the beginning of a process that can never be brought to an end, a process which . . . may be characterized

as an infinite regress. (ibid., pp. 117–118)

Therefore, in order not to get bogged down when we begin a new theory, we must of necessity leave certain terms and concepts undefined or explained. In scientific language, terms of this type are simply referred to as "primitive." The fact of the existence of primitives in the above sense does not contradict or undermine what was said earlier about not taking word meanings for granted. The idea of primitives has to do with having to *start somewhere*, while already being in the possession—a priori—of a substantial quantity and quality of knowledge, and to avoid permitting the entrance of an infinite regress. As bizarre or incredible as it initially may seem, the above procedure informs the development of the most rigorous of scientific disciplines. In Tarski's words:

> When we set out to construct a given discipline, we distinguish first of all, a certain small group of expressions of this discipline that seem to us to be immediately understandable; the expressions of this group we call primitive term or undefined terms, and we employ them without explaining their meanings . . . We proceed similarly with respect to the asserted [my emphasis] statements of the discipline under consideration. Some of these statements, which to us have the appearance of evidence, are chosen as the so-called primitive statements or axioms . . . we accept them as true without in any way establishing their validity. (ibid., p. 118)

The reader must recognize that the above comments acknowledge that science itself is based on faith. In mathematics, for example, the aforementioned primitive terms and asserted concepts—axioms—are used to develop the definitions of the discipline. The definitions are then combined with the axioms and used in turn to develop the theorems to be proved. The proofs of the theorems and their relevant examples, together with the definitions and axioms, combine to make up the substance of the discipline. When a given discipline or science is viewed from the vantage point of primitive terms, the construction along the foundation of our most rigorous of sciences, logic and mathematics, is based on nothing other than blind faith. The present work is logically rigorous in the same sense being described here. I mention these things so the reader can appreciate, despite my attempt at as casual a style as possible, my method is based on time-honored scientific practices.

The trouble with reading formal works from scratch—either as primary or even secondary sources—is one literally has to read hundreds of books before one is able to adequately discern the depth and breadth of what is being discussed. Reading is no different than any other mode of human experience. One can never read all the books that are written; therefore, vicarious experience is just as valid with respect to the body of literary experience as it is in regard to social relations in general. So ultimately it comes down to the quality and not the quantity of our literary experience, which turns out to be the most valuable. I have come to appreciate, having read hundreds of books early on, that most of the books merely allowed me to know what particular authors were saying. Obviously, what I gleaned from a few of those singular authors—as primary sources—was quite original and profound. However, a wider vision and deeper level of understanding has come to me as a result of my reading a few short and very refined formal works, and my initiating a "study" of much of the Holy Bible.

I was somewhat precocious in my youth and would occasionally sit around and ponder what other people I knew were possibly doing, at instantaneous moments in time, when they were out of my presence. For some odd reason, I came to believe while I personally could not know what others were doing when they were beyond my natural range of observation others somehow had a way of knowing everything I did when alone. I recall I even did things to test this hypothesis, but I really do not recall what the test procedures were so I cannot put my finger on why I believed what I believed back then. I now simply characterize it as intuition. ("From a child thou hast known the holy scriptures, which are able to make thee wise unto salvation through faith" [2 Tim 3:15].) My basic belief that my actions and thoughts were both constantly being monitored by others, in human form, never really left me. In fact, these thoughts would spontaneously recur from time to time. Yet if it were true, this notion that others can know my personal thoughts would *truly* be a phenomenon. The above character of thought is what David Matza (1969) refers to as a "mood of transparency." He suggests it is merely what people come to imagine to be happening, and thus they exhibit predictable *behavioral patterns* as a consequence of these ruminations (ibid., pp. 150–5.) Nowadays, based on my "personal knowledge" and experience, I can affirm this phenomenon really does exist, albeit at present I cannot prove it rigorously.[1] Now before one dismisses my comments as hocus-pocus or as being bizarre, remind oneself that the idea of something objectively being a phenomenon, by its very definition, suggests something seemingly impossible. Anyone who, for example, has ever experienced a "déjà vu"—the momentary feeling that a real time experience has actually been experienced before—can appreciate what I mean when I say, one can know a phenomenon exists but yet be unable to prove its existence. I can appreciate one's skepticism! One has first to come to believe it! That is, one has to accept it as a matter of faith, or know it as personal-knowledge based on personal experience, before this taken-for-granted impossibility can be conceived as possible at all. Nonetheless, in this book it is not my intention or purpose to discuss in extended detail this and other related phenomena. What I am prepared to discuss and even demonstrate are the mysteries of language—the word—which can lead one to what could then result in their discovery, on a personal level, of these kinds of phenomena. Only a developed "sense ability" can put the reader in touch with these phenomena. I will continue my earlier discussion of "sensibility," as being both phonetically and practically equivalent to the idea of "sense ability," in the next chapter.

On quite another conceptual level, in graduate school I began to notice, while in discussions on Marxism, the resident so-called Marxists often appeared to distort or misrepresent what Karl Heinrich Marx had written. Frequently, their comments appeared simply to be tailored to fit their own agenda. I could recognize these ploys because, as suggested by my instructors, I actually read many of Marx's original works, and some of the voluminous works of Marx's mentor Georg Wilhelm Frederick Hegel. ("Be ye doers of the word, and not just hearers only, deceiving your own selves" [Jam 1:22].) As a result of these inveterate misrepresentations, I began paying even closer attention to what people in general would be saying. It was puzzling to me how people could routinely and audaciously alter a fact when the verification of the fact could so easily be obtained and known. By paying closer attention to what people said, I began to notice something unusual. In a variety of situations, I noticed how people I knew intimately would seem to be discussing matters, in my presence and in everyday terms; but often, understanding what they actually meant was somehow beyond my grasp. It was "as if" there were two languages in one being spoken. What one might have considered as being fictional was, for me, no longer a fiction. Whether I wanted to accept it or not, there they were, common words with hidden meanings on the tips of people's tongues. It became patently clear to me there was a secret layer of meaning in the communications going on between people happening in my very presence, and at the time, I was powerless to penetrate the lexicon. Neither was what I was listening to predominately slang. Hindsight tells me, for the most part, it was the application of the subtleties in their usage of the English language that made understanding difficult. In a word, they were using "English" on me. Additionally, I could tell by the verbal posturing no one participating in those dialogues suspected I had the ability to discern an inkling of what was going on, much less have some ability to interpret what was actually being communicated.

As a result of these experiences, I determined to commit my studies to getting to the bottom of it all. ("Whosoever looketh into the perfect law of liberty [the acquisition of knowledge], and continueth therein, he being not a forgetful hearer, but a doer of the work, this man shall be blessed in his deed" [Jam 1:25].)

In this effort, while yet a graduate student, I selected the "Sociology of Knowledge" as one of four areas for specialized study. Of course, sociology, generally speaking, is the study of mankind and *everything* mankind does including all of mankind's socially constructed institutions and their practices. The Sociology of Knowledge then, in its broadest interpretation, is the study of everything that passes for the knowledge which mankind possesses. I believed that by focusing on this particular area of sociology, I stood an excellent chance of answering the questions I had about all esoteric aspects of language. As I began to uncover things and understand things in this regard, what oppressed me most was my not having any idea of the scope of my efforts; that is, what there was out there for me to know. ("I will be wise; but it was far from me. That which is far off, and exceedingly deep, who can find it out? I applied mine heart to know, and to search, and to seek out wisdom, and the reason of things, and to know the wickedness of folly, even of foolishness and madness" [Eccles. 7:23–25]). What had been the bane of my effort, up to a point, was a comment I heard someone make regarding knowledge of higher forms of knowing in general, to the effect: "Those who know don't tell, those who tell don't know!" Unfortunately, because the statement's true intended meaning is not anchored to anything substantial, there are numerous pejorative meanings which can be attributed to this comment including, for example, the notion that those who know should not tell, and others should not identify with or associate with those who do tell. That is, don't claim to know those who tell, and treat them as pariahs or outcasts. It is the perpetuation of the common immature, shallow and hackneyed notion of a "snitch." Many years have come and gone since I last permitted myself to be intimidated and distracted by what I came to interpret as a mean- spirited and deceitful if not ignorant comment. I literally had to purge my mind of this verbal demon before I could continue to develop my understanding! ("As they went out, behold, they brought to him a dumb man possessed with a demon. And when the demon was cast out, the dumb spoke; and the multitudes marveled, saying, it was never so seen in Israel" [Matt. 9:32–33].)

In fact, I now view the comment "those who know don't tell, those who tell don't know" for what it truly is, a palpable absurdity. ("We have also a more sure word of prophecy; whereunto ye do well that ye take heed, as unto a light that shineth in a dark place, until the day dawn, and the day star arise in your hearts: knowing this first, that no prophesy of the scripture [anything written] is of any private interpretation. For the prophecy came not in old time by the will of man: but holy men of God spake as they were moved by the Holy Ghost" [2 Pet 1:19–21].)

Anyone who actually believes it is wrong to discuss sacred matters, and who is not aware the dialogue on these matters is in fact ongoing, albeit often cloaked, is deluding oneself and should perish the thought. Those who are truly able to see beyond the veil, clearly, to the wide open doors of the hidden wisdom will, upon first entering, understand they are obliged to keep the doors open, provided they are not simply motivated by their own selfish will and interests. The interesting paradox in revealing some aspects of the pathways to the mysteries is they will still remain mysterious, a virtual secret. No one can effectively navigate these arcane areas of knowledge without first believing, and then acquiring and operating in sincere biblically informed faith. Otherwise, no matter what you can do on your own, much more will necessarily remain hidden from you. Much of what is hidden is based on personal knowledge—or self-knowledge, if you will—which, in the average person, is knowledge taken for granted. As personal- knowledge, much of what one gets out of all of this will depend on what one is capable of putting into it. Personal-knowledge is not simply knowledge of self, but additionally, it is the extent of one's individual knowledge about the intimate facts of our everyday world. Only the Holy Spirit possesses this kind of knowledge perfectly and completely.[2] Consequently, we are dependent on the Holy Spirit to educate us about the nuances of language and symbolism, which lead us to an understanding of sacred wisdom. Whether one chooses to accept it on not, the Holy Spirit is more than a metaphor. The Holy Spirit is real in the world! It is yet another phenomenon, which can only truly be known through experience! The reader shall soon begin to notice he or she is a participant-observer of this reality. The individual does not have to experience the Holy Spirit to gain insight into these matters, but one does need the help of the Holy Spirit to appropriately grow in the wisdom. Once one "experiences" the Holy Spirit as more than a metaphor, one will also simultaneously discover and perhaps even fully appreciate why the Bible is one of the most important books known to mankind. This is a fact, which applies, in the most objective sense, to both the believer and the non-believer alike. The Bible provides the reader, especially once it begins to be understood within the context of the present work, with the most perfect practical understanding of how to deal with the realities of ourselves and our everyday lives. One's failure to acknowledge the inescapable connection between the everyday affairs of life and biblical verse is due in part to complacency. ("So then, faith cometh by hearing, and hearing by the word of God" [Rom 10: 17].)

Certainly, there are people who are concerned about what will happen when the information and thus thoughts, erroneously considered privileged, get introduced into a wider public arena. They wonder whether or not the information will give some special interest groups an unfair advantage over others, especially the average person on the street.

Believe it or not, the correct answer is an emphatic and unequivocal honest comment to the effect, no one truly knows! However, I am personally convinced these revelations will actually go a long way toward the elimination of the already extant unfair advantages across the board. In fact, such is my intent and hope! The current perspectives are being introduced to help clear up the existing misconceptions. No matter, one must realize there is a by-product to every action. It is the action's "unintended consequences" (Merton, 1957, p. 63). Any attempt at definitively second-guessing the outcomes issuing from this exposition would be far too complex, futile, and beyond the scope of this book. It should certainly be obvious one can only act on knowledge obtained. No matter what seemingly negative effects will obtain from this effort, there will undoubtedly be positive outcomes as well (Leibnitz, 1994). Positive outcomes can immediately be translated into growth factors and the facilitation of intellectual and emotional growth is what we must concern ourselves with here.

Various historical individuals, as well as groups of people, were reported to have improved upon the knowledge they acquired. For example, in one of the most popular quotes attributed to Sir Isaac Newton, he is said to have credited his success in various scientific endeavors to having "stood on the shoulders of giants" (Boyer, 1968, p. 392). The Greeks, in leaving us a most incredible intellectual and literary legacy, are acknowledged to have "quickened" all the knowledge they acquired from other civilizations despite their refusal to supply the "historically" appropriate recognition to their sources. As the writer Carl B. Boyer (ibid.) shares with us: "The Greeks were far from hesitant in taking over elements of foreign cultures, else they could never have learned so quickly how to advance beyond their [own] predecessors, but everything they touched, they quickened" (ibid., p. 45). In fact, it is obvious the Greeks made a concerted effort to purge their records of identifying elements of origin regarding methods and original historical sources. Moreover, it appears they developed a habit of mind and the linguistic strategies whereby they could systematically accomplish this purpose. As Thomas Health (1912) informs us, after the recovery of some unusually informative manuscripts of Archimedes:

> The Method, so happily recovered, is of the greatest interest for the following reason. Nothing is more characteristic of the classical works of great geometers of Greece, or more tantalizing, than the absence of any indication of the steps by which they worked their way to the discovery of their great theorems. As they have come down to us, these theorems are finished masterpieces which leave no traces of any rough-hewn stage, no hint of the method by which they evolved (ibid., p. 6).

Heath goes on to say:

> They seem to have taken pains to clear away all traces of the machinery used all the litter, so to speak, resulting from tentative efforts, before they permitted themselves to publish, in sequence carefully thought out, and with definitive and rigorously scientific proofs, the results obtained (ibid., p. 7).

Using this approach or style for public presentation of intellectual materials, the Greeks need not have acted in a "spirit of fear" (2 Tim 1:7) with respect to using a written as opposed to an oral tradition of handing down information over generations.[3] By "abstracting" (Johnson, 1946, pp. 143–169) the facts and data from their historical foundations and details, the Greeks masked all direct informative roads to their wisdom and its varied original sources. In other words, they taught themselves how to and devised ways of controlling the dissemination of knowledge, while yet being able to maintain a workable and retrievable historical record. As developed, the skill of cloaking selected facts in secrecy which the Greeks succeeded in quickening, even if nothing else would be said about their prowess, was the Greek's special genius and habit of mind. Their efforts facilitated a masking of any direct or immediate insight into the deeper original elements of knowledge. For me, it has been intellectually instructive and in the interest of my own growth in learning to presuppose a more expanded genius and a more open habit of mind existed before the Greeks, and much of it and its historical record has been hidden from us, even lost. I assumed if I could encourage and then persuade my mind to imagine this scenario as the probable even likely one, I would be able to establish a mental and emotional state of mind which possibly would enable me to rediscover. using my imagination, some of the lost wisdom and specific knowledge. Hegel explains this somewhat technical procedure in the following way:

> Only by turning the entire process upside down does the whole thing get its right relationship in which the connexion (sic) of ground and consequent, and the correctness of the transformation of perception into thought can be surveyed. Hence one of the chief difficulties in the study of such sciences is to *effect an entrance into them*; and this can only be done if the presuppositions are *blindly taken* for granted, and straightway, without being able to form any Notion of them, in fact with barely a definite representation but at most a confused picture in the imagination, to impress upon one's memory for the time being the determinations of the assumed forces and matters, and their hypothetical formations, directions and rotations. If, in order to accept these presuppositions as valid, we demand their necessity and their Notion, we cannot get beyond the starting point. (Hegel, 1969, p. 815)

The kind of mental construct or mind-set I adopted, and which is being referred to is a type of mental "autonomy" or even intellectual detachment, if you will, from what we are conventionally used to thinking. Whenever this kind of emotional and intellectual suspension of and departure from taken-for-granted ways of thinking can be established, a mental environment for creative thought can come into existence. The following quote will help inform the idea I wish to infuse here. As Peter Berger (1963) observes:

> A man who passionately devotes his life to the study of pure mathematics [for example] can afford to pay a minimum of attention to routine social demands, as long as he can somehow manage to survive economically in the pursuit of his interests. And, what is more important, the directions of thinking that these universes of discourse will naturally lead him to will have a very high degree of autonomy indeed vis-à- vis the routine intellectual patterns that constitute the worldview of man's society. One may recall here the toast delivered at a gathering of mathematicians: "To pure mathematics—and may it never be of any use to anybody!" . . . this kind of sub world does not arise out of rebellion against society as such, but it leads all the same to an autonomous intellectual universe within which an individual can exist with almost Olympic detachment. Put differently, it is possible for men, alone or in groups, to construct their own worlds [intellectually] and on this basis to detach themselves from the world into which they were originally socialized. (ibid., p. 133)

Berger is even suggesting that these kinds of mental constructs are the gifts of the economically privileged because one has to be able to *afford* the *time* for these ruminations.

The Greeks systematically established this kind of mental autonomy for themselves, and through it designed a new intellectual firmament to suit their whim and caprice, one which was to be esoterically habituated, in a form capable of being continued even extended down through the ages. In its most formal attire, we have come to know it, in varying forms, as the "scientific method." The only way to get inside this realm, if you will, of learning and/or representation is to usurp this construct of mental autonomy, and then focus one's thoughts within a pre-historical perspective for the sole purpose of interpreting history by means of interpolation. In other words, there are times when one will, for the sake of the argument, simply have to "guess" what the answer to his/her query might possibly be, and only then seek to establish the facts in objective terms. Mathematicians are often obliged to "conjecture," that is, guess, in their effort to grow the knowledge in diverse areas of the discipline (Long, 1987, pp. 8–10). Placed within a historical context, mental autonomy and guessing amount to the active notion of presupposition.

Since so much of the praise given to the Greeks springs from their contributions in mathematics and philosophy, historical excursions within these two subjects have afforded me a substantial amount of atypical insight. The reader must clearly understand that:

> There can be no sharp boundary between the history of a subject and the subject itself. The only difference can be of emphasis, or of focus of interest. The reason is simple: the existing theories or theorems are not only statements of fact, but they are also solutions to problems . . . the old problems are as much a guide to our research as the theories, which solved them. (W. Berkson, 1976, p. 47)

In other words, in order for one to know what to do or to know what was done, one must have a clear idea of what is actually going on or what actually went on in regard to the original problem. The

Greeks in their time did not and, as part of that legacy and living tradition, modern mathematics does not routinely afford the learner a fair glimpse into what is actually going on in the discipline, before posing problems for the learner to attempt to solve.[4] As William Berkson (ibid.) has suggested:

> Mathematics textbooks would be a hundred times easier to understand if they were three times longer—if they contained the other two-thirds of the subjects they discuss. Now the student is forced to reinvent the other two-thirds for himself. This closes the subject to all but those who have both this particular gift, and the knowledge that it [the historical review] has to be done, and the interest to do it.[5] Now mathematics is usually taught either by the rote method, driving in somehow mechanical skills with a minimum of understanding, or taught by "new" methods which try to give the latest up-to-date formal version, whose concepts have been stretched beyond the understanding of most who do not already know the earlier version of the subject and the connection of its mechanics to recent modifications. (ibid., pp. 48–49)

Many students of higher mathematics, in particular, will fall as victim to this real-time experience and pattern of deception. It is a pattern of activity I have personally observed within the discipline. As a consequence, the pattern has informed what I have come to believe is the intended meaning and/or the politically convenient adaptation of the expression "method of exhaustion." This was the phraseology as concept used by Archimedes and applied by him within the context of his geometrical constructions (Heath, 1912). However, the expression is consistent with the notion of weeding out people. That is, many students of formal mathematics become "exhausted" from the unnatural exigencies of trying to master the subject. They become disenchanted with the subject because of what in the end is an artificially imposed abstruseness in higher mathematics, and consequently, many are found to abandon any further formal study in advanced mathematics. Mathematics is difficult enough without having to have more levels of difficulties deliberately implanted within it. Hence, advanced mathematics stands as one of the prime examples of how the "old boy" network works.[6] No matter, it should soon become obvious that with the appropriate keys, the subject of mathematics and its politics has been and can be rendered as transparent as that within any other discipline.

The above revelations notwithstanding, I have discovered in this study that it is the Holy Spirit who rightly quickens all knowledge. As Hegel informs us:

> Since man has in language a means of designation peculiar to Reason, it is idle fancy to search for a less perfect mode of representation to plague oneself with. It is essentially only spirit that can comprehend the Notion as Notion; for this is not merely the property of spirit but spirit's pure self. It is futile to seek to fix it by spatial figures and algebraic signs for the purpose of the outer eye and an uncomprehending, mechanical mode of treatment such as a calculus. In fact, anything else which might be supposed to serve as a symbol can at most, like symbols for the nature of God, evoke intimations and echoes of the Notion; if, however, one should seriously propose to employ them for expressing and cognizing the Notion, then the external nature of all symbols is inadequate to the task; the truth about the relationship is rather the converse, namely, that what in symbols is an echo of a higher determination, is only truly known through the Notion and can be approximated to the Notion only by separating-off the sensuous, unessential part that was meant to express it. (Hegel, 1969, p. 618)

The entity that gives us, in Hegelian terms (ibid.), a "notion of the notion," which we need and are ever trying to capture is different in kind from the symbols and language the entity helps us create and use to try and describe itself. Spirit is the notion. The notion is a spirit. No symbols used with the intent of dressing it up to impress, no fixing it in some visual aesthetic, no symbolic mystification can possibly represent what spirit is. What spirit does for us is it comprehends itself, the notion, and gives us our footing and compass as relates to our having a sense of that which we can only have a notion. Spirit mediates our will. The words we use are an echo of spirit. ("It is the spirit that quickens; the flesh profiteth nothing: the words that I speak unto you, they are spirit and they are life" [Joh 6:63].) Moreover, as we are currently uncovering them, it is the Holy Spirit alone who can guide us safely into and through the mysteries. My comment about safety here is very real. ("As also in all his epistles, speaking in them of these things; in which are some things hard to be understood, which they that are unlearned and unstable wrest, as they do also the other scriptures, unto their destruction. Ye therefore, beloved, seeing ye know these things before, beware lest ye also, being led away with the error of the wicked [acting as if this knowledge is a matter of personal will alone], fall from your own steadfastness (sic)" [2 Pet 3:16–17].) On their excursion into the mysteries, the unguided will necessarily tiptoe on a fine line, the line that separates sanity and insanity. Without a seasoned guide, the uninitiated can become emotionally "unsteady" or lose his/her emotional steadfastness and intellectual bearings, even "go off the deep end," so to speak. Thus one is exposed to yet another purpose of the present book, and that is to help protect the readers who, through independent study, might have inadvertently found themselves on the path to what an earlier quote referred to as the "wickedness of folly, even of foolishness and madness." My immediate comments are intended as a safety precaution informing the reader these are serious matters. It poses the possibility it may well be "wicked" to even consider guiding anyone along the road to the discovery of the mysteries. In honest deference, I say to the present reader, I will not be offended if the reader chooses to abandon the effort. In other words, if the reader at some point chooses to abandon any further reading and study of this work, and related materials. It is not my intention to expose you to wickedness on any level, but I will admit a review of the content of this book, and its related materials, is risky business for the neophyte. That one pursues the good and has good intentions does not necessarily imply good results in every case. These are essentially esoteric materials, and the subject matter can run the gamut from the vilest to the most sublime and holy. However, my effort is to place the reader in the middle range of possible meanings, thus giving the topics as much balance as is possible. To this end, having assured myself the reader is well grounded I have then revealed only some and only just enough of the "what can suggest the much more" to the reader. That is, at best one can still only be provided with a notion of the notion. This will come primarily in the form of the anagrammatic examples given in chapter four. In other words, it is my intent that the reader's potential further development in this area of knowledge, beyond what is immediately developed in the present work, remain squarely placed in the reader's own hands, and in a way that is manageable and not problematic. This is the principal value in my utilizing the anagram as technique and it is an appropriate way to render the latent information contained in any written statement open for review and general use. Of course, we have a conventional definition of what an anagram is, but that definition only represents a version of my actual representation of an anagram. One will discover there is an in-kind or qualitative difference in what I will represent as an anagram and what one's prior or initial notion was of the anagram.

What will be given more often than not will only comply with the notion of what is an anagram. Technically, they will be anagrams in spirit. Let it be clear, I am not representing myself in place of the Holy Spirit. I am merely sharing some stages of my personal development, as informed by the Holy Spirit. In my effort to learn how to explain this knowledge, I had some amorphous idea of a need for a special device, and the Holy Spirit answered my will, in a step-by-step manner, by directing my understanding to the anagram. There is an irony in Hegel's expose on this aspect of knowledge. Hegel explains in extended detail every aspect of the nature, character, and purpose of an anagram, without calling it by that name (ibid., pp. 576–844).

I think it instructive to share with the reader some facts regarding my personal emotional reactions to these matters. In doing so, I must confess that emotionally it has not been a trouble-free encounter even for me. I attribute the difficulty primarily to my finding myself always having to work on these matters alone while breaking new ground. Many years ago, while I was yet formally an active graduate student, my attempts to obtain guidance on these matters from academicians resulted in my coming into contact with principally three types of individuals. Those who claimed to know absolutely nothing of these things, those who were "said" to know nothing about the matter, and those who acknowledged knowing but postured that the understanding of these matters, on their deeper levels, were not to be discussed openly. Furthermore, those of the latter type encouraged me to be careful not to enlighten certain individuals we had mutual involvement with at the time. In particular, they were referring to the so-called Marxists I mentioned earlier. Moreover, they would themselves not enter into any further detailed discussion of the matter with me; albeit I had noted they were among the individuals who I previously mentioned appeared to actively utilize the knowledge in conversation. By the way, I too, after all these years. occasionally make casual use of this technique of intellectual nuance in conversation. It turns out to be an almost natural and at times appropriate by-product of a heightened consciousness.

Even though I was searching for them, I had initially stumbled onto these insights into language and its usage and was then startled and traumatized by what I found with respect to the total experience surrounding my discovery. In his seminal work entitled *Becoming Deviant*, David Matza (1969) uses the metaphor of a "marijuana user" when effectively detailing the experience I am referring to here (ibid., p. 109). In his words, what I personally experienced was "Ban: being bedeviled" (ibid., p. 146). As a result of the negative reactions from those I approached on the subject, I began believing the research I was involved in was considered a banned or criminal activity. Consequently, I began experiencing the guilt, fear, and other negative internal reactions associated with that kind of belief. The peculiar thing about the presumptively banned activity was it could not be strictly determined to be illegal in the everyday sense of criminal activity. There were no overt extant laws to be found which forbade the activity. However, when I initiated discussions on the matter with others, the experience was such that I was repeatedly left with the inescapable impression that the activity was something tacitly forbidden.[7] As Matza states:

> That ban imbues an activity with guilt is hardly surprising or unintentional. The moral transformation of activity is the purpose of ban; the simplest way of summarizing the . . . purportedly public attention [my emphasis] is to predict that with time the activity will exist in guilt. (ibid.)

Matza is telling us the phenomenon of "ban" exists for the *purpose* of expressing moral indignation thus causing the individual to experience moral consternation over certain activities, and with the intent of altering one's moral outlook and thus actual behavior. Speaking from my personal experience in these matters, I trust the reader will believe me when I say I can attest to the fact that the "attention" [noticing, believing, and accepting that one is actually being quietly observed] is not just "purportedly." The public attention of which Matza speaks has in my experience been very real, not imagined. The interesting thing is there is no way of determining when the observing or monitoring of one's intellectual pursuits first begins. One might ask, at what instance does an individual's seemingly innocent activities become an issue? According to Matza:

> So immersed is the subject in the context of state that no sequence in the appearance of issues can be posited. Issues simply appear and a resolution must be devised by the subject as he continues his still ordinary life within a society regulated by a state that has chosen to ban something he is doing. (ibid., p. 149)

The above notwithstanding, Matza suggests:

> This need not mean that the guilt of banned activity inevitably rubs off on the subjects or that they do not eventually get over their initial trepidation and unease; but it does indicate a number of manifest tendencies and thus matters to be considered by the attentive subject. That the guilt of banned activity maybe managed or perhaps even neutralized testifies to the eventual capacity of the subject and not to the inconsequentiality of the sovereign's [the state] intention. (ibid., p. 146)[8]

What precisely is it we are witnessing here within his statements? Matza is admitting the "attention" is actual or real; yet, perhaps only noticed by the "attentive subject." In fact, he states, it is "the sovereign's intention" the subject individual notices the attention. As mentioned earlier, it is actually a form of hazing. It is designed to foster the kind of introspection, which will influence, if not completely alter, one's behavior. To cause one to stop doing the banned thing. Thus the subject person's actions and reactions become the obvious and anticipated items of scrutiny. He additionally acknowledges it is within the "capacity" of the subject individual, in time, to learn to cope with or emotionally adjust to the reality of being under scrutiny. In the interim, the subject's behavior is simply monitored. He further observes that:

> The consequences of ban may be manifold [many] and mixed [varied] but their serious consideration requires that we begin with the phenomenon, as it morally exists— guilty. Only when that is granted may the social responses of participating subjects be traced. (ibid.)

In other words, the so-called "guilty" subject begins exhibiting a predictably revealing and traceable pattern of behavior. Matza is also indicating that the subject individual who simply manages to persevere through the intimidation, by simply continuing in the activity despite the state's tacit intention, has actually undergone a transition and become part of the game. The individual will in effect have reached a resolution of the issues in the character of acting on a higher level of a participating subject by being able to manage the initial feelings of guilt. Personally, I am one of those who have learned to cope with the scrutiny, which, in real-time experience, is actually an *earning* of the right to cope with the scrutiny. Thus, one simply becomes the deviant, that is, evolves into the appropriate behavioral patterns of the deviant characterization. Meaning the person necessarily becomes, within *prudent* limits, defiant and, in time, continues following a constructively productive existence.

One must be careful here to understand this becoming is not a bad or evil act. On the contrary, it is a tremendous intellectual feat. It is a significant achievement. In the end, one basically learns to respond appropriately to the most obvious indicators. In other words, one learns, as best one can, how to read the signs. They are signs that direct individuals away from the highly sensitive information in regard to the most critical of state secrets. It is the sociological conception of a person becoming more thoroughly human (ibid., p. 109). As a by-product of the experience, one will in fact have acquired a greater ability to handle the everyday affairs of life since, in the process, the social and intellectual parameters become better well defined. ("Because the worshipers once purged should have . . . no more consciousness of sins" [Heb. 10:2].) Matza has indicated that to survive the above intimidation in any normal manner is not the typical outcome. In a footnote attached to the last quotation, Matza discusses the typical prognosis for an individual who experiences this kind of bewilderment:

> The usual fate of participants in banned activity is much more prosaic: their consciousness never expands or otherwise develops. (ibid., p. 147)

It is being suggested that an individual can either become oblivious or learn to persevere under any feelings of guilt. Thus the person never wallows in guilt, learns to cope with feeling of guilt, or the experience can be so tainted in guilt it can permanently disable the individual thus thwarting any emotional and intellectual growth beyond the immediate trauma. The subject then can get caught in an emotional loop, ranging from guilt and bewilderment to feeling like a pariah. I will hint that the kinds of activities and topics whose exploration can exist in guilt, under our current reflection, as those having either a sensuous or semiotic orientation. The sensuous side has to do with the process of adult maturation mentioned earlier. It can be culturally based and relates directly and specifically to one's social and sexual habits. The semiotic side concerns one's involvement in cryptographic research. Put simply, for many of us, our activities as willful adults are often monitored by the state. Whether we like it or not, the state can monitor our individual formal intellectual research activities and our social habits at their discretion, and we have absolutely no say in the matter. Additionally, it is important to point out, either one of these contexts has the power to awaken an individual's self- consciousness to being the subject of this attention. As the person involved, one becomes mindful of one's potential or actual "transparency" (ibid., pp. 150–155). I can describe the intensity of the initial sensation of transparency. It is like what one would likely experience were he/she in total darkness to secret himself/herself onto the center of the fifty-yard line in a football stadium, and suddenly have all the stadium lights turned on you revealing a stadium full of spectators. I imagine it being on the order of the nakedness Adam and Eve are alleged to have felt after eating the forbidden fruit of the Garden of Eden. That is, as Matza tells us:

> Being bedeviled is an inner experience though its outward manifestations enhance the deviant subject's adaptation to social control. (ibid., p. 149)

It is important enough to re-emphasize activities that focus on the intellectual treatment of sensuous behavior, and those that examine semiotic contents, are among the things which at times are subject to state scrutiny. The reason for the state's concern is that both these subject areas have traditionally been considered to broach on state secrets. It is the kind of information typically provided only on a "need-to-know" basis and once would even have included our present discussion. Thus guilt is supposed to act as the deterrent to one's participation in the morally guilty activity. It is intended to cause one to stop doing what he/she is doing or planning to do in the above regard. Thus, it often does, as it is designed to do, result in lifestyle changes. Guilt, as it is portrayed here, is then the conspicuous agent of social control. Yet the subject may or may not adapt. The idea of adaptation implies a stabilizing influence. It is the real-time activity of learning to manage what potentially could have been overwhelming, a deliberately awakened sense of fear. However, the very essence of bedevilment is emotional instability. For example, bedevilment often happens to graduate students when they begin making serendipitous discoveries in the higher levels of knowing and meaning. It can be an emotionally traumatic time for the student. I would bet many volumes could be filled with the emotional anecdotes of these kinds of experiences. This should not be a time to abandon the student. It could instead be a time for closer observation for the purpose of nurturing. There is absolutely no reason why graduate education should not be a love feast. Be assured that for many it is not! Contrary to its popular and projected image, the college environment is not necessarily user friendly in many cases. Since bedevilment produces behavior which is traceable, I can see no justifiable reason why, in every instance, someone could not be standing in the breach to pull the bedeviled person back from the brink; rather than promoting their wandering out to "sea," so to speak (Foucault, 1961). People need others to be concerned and advisedly supportive when they claim the stairs to higher learning and turn the key to the door of even deeper levels of knowing. Someone could and should be there willing to offer them guidance and an emotionally stabilizing influence. We must recognize true bedevilment is a state of absolute confusion and fear. As such, it is the stuff of a real potential for tragedy. God only knows how many homicides, suicides, complete emotional breakdowns, and other related tragedies could be averted were the state to adopt a slightly different posture in this regard. In contrast, I believe God intends for us to help our fellowman not simply lord over him. ("Brethren, if a man be overtaken in a fault, ye which are spiritual, restore such an one in the spirit of meekness; considering thyself, lest thou also be tempted. Bear ye one another's burdens, and so fulfill the law of Christ. For if a man thinks himself to be something, when he is nothing, he deceiveth himself. But let every man prove his own work, and then shall he have rejoicing in himself alone, and not in another. For every man shall bear his own burden. Let him that is taught in the word communicate unto him that teacheth in all good things. Be not deceived; God is not mocked: for whatsoever a man soweth, that shall he also reap" [Gal. 6:1–7]). I believe appropriate persons in the house [academe and the church] are supposed to be there and willing to try and protect the neophyte and laity, guiding them through the "labyrinth" of the personal-knowledge revelations many of them will experience. How else will one be able to stay the emotional roller coaster which is the inevitable by-product of stumbling onto these higher consciousness levels, without the benefit of prior substantive tutelage. To provide direct tutelage, by way of sharing aspects of my personal experience, reveals yet another pertinent reason for the production of this book. The Bible expresses this maelstrom of human experience in the following way:

> For we know that the law is spiritual, but I am carnal, sold under sin. For that which I do I allow not: for what I would, that do I not; but what I hate, that do I. If then I do that which I would not, I consent unto the law that it is good. Now then it is no more I that do it, but sin that dwelleth in me. For I know that in me (that is, in my flesh) dwelleth no good thing: for to will is present with me; but how to perform that which is good I find not. For the good that I would I do not: but the evil, which I would not, that I do. Now if I do that I would not, it is no more I that do it, but sin that dwelleth in me. I find then a law, that, when I would do good, evil is present with me. For I delight in the law of God after the inward man: But I see another law in my members, warring against the law of my mind, and bringing me into captivity to the law of sin which is in my members. O wretched man that I am! Who shall deliver me from the body of this death? I thank God through Jesus Christ our Lord. So then with the mind I myself serve the law of God; but with the flesh the law of sin. (Rom 7:14–25)

It should be obvious with the inclusion of the above quote that it is my intention that the present work not only be read but also studied. It also points to the fact we can find the best in ourselves if we can develop the capability of hearing, and then adopt the willingness with the patience to listen to our own inner spirits. There is always a tension existing between what we know and what we feel. Moreover, because feelings often come and go as they please there is a limit to both moral and political sanctions. I consider myself somewhat fortunate to have overcome the above maelstrom and to be in a position of knowing I am now emotionally and intellectually secure. ("Brethren, I count not myself to have apprehended: but this one thing I do, forgetting those things which are behind, and reaching forth unto those things which are before" [Phil. 3:13].) In my opinion, to have originally been left in a position to inevitably stumble onto this kind of insight, without the benefit of the appropriate prior tutelage or real time mediation is a generational curse.

Of course the text as I have expanded it sounds somewhat religious, and not like the social science discourse initially claimed. Perish the thought that I am found to be proselytizing! I am only stating the facts as I have discovered them. Nonetheless—and I have deliberately taken pains to make it obvious with my parenthetical notes—the facts do have biblical contexts and references. Thus, as exposition, I remain the objective participant observer of the truth. The famous theorist Karl Mannheim (1936) does an excellent job of explaining what I mean by objectivity here, when he states:

> If the earlier discussion of objectivity laid stress upon the elimination of personal and collective bias, the more modern approach calls attention to the positive cognitive importance of this bias. Whereas the former quest for objectivity tended to posit an "object" which was distinct from the "subject," the latter sees an intimate relationship

between the object and the perceiving subject. In fact, the most recent view maintains that the object emerges for the subject when, in the course of experience, the interest of the subject is focused upon that particular aspect of the world. (ibid., p. xvii)

Mannheim is saying that with respect to the issue of scientific objectivity, there is a new game in town. No longer is the researcher limited to and obliged to be emotionally detached from the object of his or her research. That is, as Mannheim informs us:

whereas objectivity in the first sense refers to the reliability of our data and the validity of our conclusions, objectivity in the second sense is concerned with relevance to our interests. In the realm of the social . . . truth is not merely a matter of a simple correspondence between thought and existence, but is tinged with the investigator's interest in his subject matter, his standpoint, his evaluations, in short the definition of his object of attention. (ibid., p. xviii)

Mannheim rounds off these comments with the following pivotal insight:

This conception of objectivity, however, does not imply that henceforth no distinction between truth and error is ascertainable. It does not mean that whatever people imagine to be their perceptions, attitude, and ideas or what they want others to believe them to be corresponds to the facts. Even in this conception of objectivity we must reckon with the distortion produced not merely by inadequate perception or incorrect knowledge of oneself, but also by the inability or unwillingness under certain circumstances to report perceptions and ideas honestly. (ibid.)

One must recognize a most peculiar truth about social science discussion. As Peter Berger (1963) so aptly informs us:

> It can be said that the first wisdom of sociology is this—things are not what they seem. This too is a deceptively simple statement. It ceases to be simple after a while. Social reality turns out to have many layers of meaning. The discovery of each new layer changes the perception of the whole. (ibid., p. 23)

One might think our discussion should lead us into quantitative and even more rigorous forms of explanation. On the contrary, we should remain attentive and grounded in everyday experience to explain the realities most immediately before us in our everyday lives. The quantitative elements will come to us, so to speak, or come to objectify themselves, once we have taken the time to expand our understanding of the qualitative aspects of knowledge. With all of the preceding essential truths in our grasp, we are ready to examine in some detail Immanuel Kant's tremendous fundamental contribution to our general understanding and to the immediate essential ways of thinking.

ENDNOTES

1   What I mean by "personal knowledge" is:

a. Knowledge known to oneself exclusively and to the extent it absolutely cannot be attested to being known by others with the same degree of intimacy. This would include knowledge gained about and by oneself through the process of sober introspection.
b. The facts that are known to oneself in general, through both formal and informal education and experience.
c. The collection of information which would reveal knowledge about one personally or individually, and which can be known by someone other than oneself, including facts not known by the subject individuals themselves.

As a point of reflection, the above items taken together represent the content of what I would more readily express as "personal-knowledge." Moreover, I believe my use of the expression "personal knowledge" is fairly synonymous with Immanuel Kant's expression "self-knowledge." Also see *Personal Knowledge* (1962) by Michael Polanyi.

2   The reader should reference the King James Version of the Bible as a definitive source of my meaning and use of the notion of Holy Spirit. Of course, the Bible at times also speaks of the Holy Ghost. The Bible might make a well-defined distinction between the entities Holy

Spirit and Holy Ghost. However, my readers should have no problem appreciating my dual usage of the name Holy Spirit.

3   That is, the Greeks *guarded against* having to have "fear" surrounding the knowledge they wished to maintain control over, to grow, to preserve, and to transmit via a formal written tradition, as opposed to an oral tradition. One should take note, a written tradition's major import is it serves to maintain the accuracy and precision of the discrete items of information, as against involuntary natural memory lapses inevitably occurring when individuals rely on an oral tradition.

4   See Hegel's book entitled *Scientific Logic* for an in-depth discussion of these issues.

5   As an educator, it is not uncommon for me to personally observe how "favored" students are coddled and even "spoon-fed," so to speak, when they run into real intellectual difficulties.

6   The following comments are revelations, based on my interpretation of the cipher contained in Leibnitz's article entitled "Monadology":

7   Liebnitz is discussing the nature and characteristics of individuals as potential mathematicians, and the politics surrounding one's official induction into what amounts to a fraternal order. He argues that anyone with the wherewithal to complete their mathematical study to the level of calculus or, in modern terms, the four-semester sequence in calculus is technically a mathematician; for all intents and purposes, with respect to one's ability and aptitude. However, he relates major growth beyond that point, which in effect is the entrance into the study of "pure" mathematics, is dependent almost exclusively on the amount of assistance one will get from journeymen mathematicians and mathematical referees. Students, he argues, cannot gain full possession

of the missing pieces of the remaining intellectual puzzles within mathematics, without direct intervention and assistance. Consequently, he establishes the point, in order for would-be pure mathematicians to become great mathematicians, they have to satisfy the criteria of a subjective selection process. And I establish this in the interpretation of an anagram developed from a statement in mathematical context, the preference goes to the fastest able learners. See the anagram "Fermats Last Theorem" in chapter four.

8   It is not coincidental, concurrent with my library-based research discoveries in the field of cryptography, the National Security Agency (NSA) began litigation in the Federal courts to be granted the legal authority to remove certain books from circulation in libraries. Specifically, their argument was individuals with strong mathematical backgrounds had the aptitude to penetrate state secrets in cryptographic procedures. As I recall, around the same time, some graduate student had been censored and his materials confiscated for having designed an actual atomic bomb on paper using information obtained from library books on the subject. The above court battle over cryptography lasted over ten years, beginning in the early 1970s and ending in the early 1980s. In the end, the NSA lost most of the rulings. However, the NSA retains the authority over the surveillance of American citizens, in contrast to the Central Intelligence Agency's (CIA) international role of surveillance of nations and individuals outside of the United States. This is all part of the public record, so I will not list any references; but, rather, I will defer to those interested readers to do their own research on these matters.

8. See *The State in a Capitalistic Society* by Ralph Miliband to review my meaning of "the state" here.

CHAPTER THREE

OF COURSE IMMANUEL KANT KNEW!

According to the grace of God which is given unto me, as a wise masterbuilder, I have laid the foundation, and another buildeth thereon. But let every man take heed how he buildeth thereupon. For other foundation can no man lay than that is laid, which is Jesus Christ.

—1 Cor. 3:10–11

PART ONE

I n this chapter I will continue exercising the writer's privilege to use extensive quotes. My purpose in doing so is to constrain the author I am referencing to explain what he has intended to say but in the fewest words possible. By this I mean, I will be short-cutting some explanations which span, if I were to include my review of the work of both Kant and Hegel, a few thousand pages of some of the most arduous texts I have ever encountered. Moreover, I am using this method because I wish to demonstrate to the reader that what I am reintroducing has been discussed at length before but primarily in elliptical terms. Additionally, I will continue and even extend my use of the device of interjecting bracketed commentary within the directed quotes, for the purpose of assisting in the flow and clarity of the dialogue.

One of the most important classic works on the subject of which I speak is Immanuel Kant's *Critique of Pure Reason* (Kant,1965). Much of what Kant wrote in the *Critique* can be arduous; that is, difficult to follow and understand. It is difficult for the neophyte to understand, not because it lacks, in Kant's terms, "clearness" but, rather, because it lacks an earthy everyday vernacular and context. It lacks this context because Kant deliberately avoided everyday examples of the objects of which he spoke. Kant even declares he could have provided us with examples of the items he is discussing yet, to my knowledge he never did. Therefore, we can only assume Kant knew how to develop examples, and thereby merely attempt to characterize his purported examples and try to imagine how his examples would have aided our understanding. Consequently, we find ourselves in a similar situation to that fostered by Fermat's Last Theorem in mathematics. Concerning the proof of an important mathematical theorem, the great mathematician Pierre de Fermat claimed he had a proof of the theorem, which he could fit into the margins of his book; however, he never actually showed the proof. Consequently, the proof eluded the best efforts of mathematicians for centuries. The theorem of which Fermat spoke was recently proven by the mathematician Andrew Wiles, and the proof itself is said to span more than two hundred pages (Aczel, 1996). Depending on one's perspective, I guess one might argue that the lengthy proof uncovered by Wiles actually could fit within the covers or "margins" of a book. Heck, I am working diligently to entail all of what I wish to say in the present book in less than two hundred pages. And within those pages to puzzle out, for the reader's benefit, the kinds of examples that Kant implied. Kant expresses his perception of the difficulty in supplying examples, as the problem of maintaining brevity of exposition, when the issue presented itself to him in his day when he says:

> I have been almost continuously at a loss, during the
> progress of my work, how I should proceed in this matter.
> Examples and illustrations seemed always to be necessary,

and so took their place, as required, in my first draft. But I very soon became aware of the magnitude of my task and of the multiplicity of matters with which I should have to deal; and as I perceived that even if treated in dry, purely scholastic fashion, the outcome would by itself be already quite sufficiently large in bulk, I found it inadvisable to enlarge it yet further through examples and illustrations. (Kant,1965, pp. 12–13)

Unlike Kant, in the present book I will use a family of examples to illustrate what is the subject matter of Kant's discussion. In fact, I have taken a completely different tact. My book is designed to pivot on these examples. I do this despite what we bear witness to in Kant's own words, where he tells us he deliberately chose not to give his readers adequate "assistance" by way of supplying "examples and illustrations" in his exposition. For he states:

These [examples and illustrations] are necessary only from a popular point of view; and this work can never be made suitable for popular consumption.

Such assistance is not required by genuine students of the science, and, though always pleasing, might very well in this case have been self-defeating in its effects. (ibid., p. 13)

On the contrary, assuming that one possesses the skill to supply adequate examples, I believe it intellectually self-defeating to not take advantage of the effective use of examples. Appropriate examples can serve to help illuminate and thereby eliminate the ostensible inconsistencies that pure theory often engenders. Kant stated that "this work can never be made suitable for popular consumption." One should not ever say this of anything that it is never possible. The level of intellectual work we are considering might not ever become a fade, on the level of popularity, but it need not be completely relegated to the esoteric either. It is clear that Kant had chosen a public that his work was designed to reach. He wished to reach "genuine students of the science," and not the everyday person. Elsewhere he is also critical of what, in his terms, would be the illegitimate monopolistic persona of a dogmatic academia (ibid., pp. 30–31). I tend to strongly agree with him on this latter point. In Kant's words, genuine students of science have the discipline, "interest" in other words, required to endure the tedium associated with mastering abstruse exposition. They are all willing to waste, in other words, the time it takes to understand material deliberately designed to be difficult to read and understand. Of course, these same students might choose a different attitude or posture toward these materials if they were to be made aware that the materials are often "deliberately" designed to waste their time. We evidence this practice, as Kant bears witness to it, when he states:

> The reader is not allowed to arrive sufficiently quickly at a conspectus [overview] of the whole; the bright colouring of the illustrative material intervenes to cover over and conceal the articulation and organisation of the system, which, if we are to be able to judge of its unity and solidity [from previous intellectual habits and styles of discourse such as the Greek legacy], are what chiefly concern us. (ibid., p. 13)

Kant indicates here that the traditional philosophy intended to promote an esoteric style of presentation. So he tacitly consents to continue the practice and process of stonewalling and forestalling direct revelation and clarity . . . in the name of maintaining a presumed traditional intent. Moreover, he understands the maintenance of this style and intent for the presentation of topics of discussion would essentially render the reading of the materials as a chore for the typical reader, and that would include even the so-called "genuine students of the science."

At this point, we need to clearly recognize what Kant wanted, and was proposing to continue. He wished to continue the traditional Greek style in formal written public discourse. The legacy left by the Greeks was to produce and fashion a discourse which would both reveal, as a complete system, some significant information while simultaneously concealing its straightforward breadth of meaning in a permanent style and in a systematic fashion for all times. But what was this substance which Kant and the Greeks before him wanted to give complete representation to yet, all the while, simultaneously concealing its elemental core? It is left for us to rediscover, but Kant unwittingly tells us:

> It [information techniques or information technology in more contemporary terms] is nothing but the inventory of all our possessions through pure reason, systematically arranged. In this field [the field of knowledge and more pointedly the field of information gathering and fact finding] nothing can escape us. What reason produces entirely out of itself [consequently] cannot be concealed, but is brought to light by reason itself immediately the common principle has been discovered. (ibid., p. 14)

This "inventory of all our possessions" refers to all that we learn and have learned through our powers of observation, discovery, and reasoning about human nature, but referenced in a concealed form away from the general public's immediate observation and understanding. He is also referring to information gathering based on simple rumination, and the general findings issuing from these ruminations as well-defined catalogued elements for our potential creativity. That is, just sitting around and thinking about the range of possible human actions and various scenarios, along with the theoretical designs of future useful physical objects. It is the "principle" of possible outcomes being imagined or thought of beforehand and introduced as an "appearance" within language even before the actual experience or action has taken place, and even before the physical object has been introduced into the physical world. I will have more to say about the meaning of the term "appearance" within this context later.

Of course, the discovery of the common principle that would routinely unveil the information of which he speaks is not necessarily an inevitable achievement whose success should be complacently taken-for-granted. The knowledge he is discussing is in a peculiar sense an uncommon kind of knowledge. That is, it is knowledge of the sort not naturally anticipated or expected given our traditional ways of thinking. Neither does it necessarily reveal itself through a common experience as Kant himself immediately admits, when he continues:

> The complete unity of this kind of knowledge, and the fact that it is derived solely from pure concepts [the kind of concepts derived by way of *presupposition*], entirely uninfluenced by any experience or by special intuition, such as might lead to any determinate experience that would enlarge and increase it, make this unconditioned completeness not only practicable but also necessary. (ibid.)

I have discovered through my own use of pure concepts, at least one "sense" of, the "common principle" in its "unconditioned completeness" of which Kant speaks. It is in every respect captured or exhibited in the concept of the anagram. Within this context, each *anagram* is to be viewed as a short or mini-proof. In his discussion of the "Notion," Hegel (1969) provides the most definitive description of what it is and the purpose of the anagram that I have ever read despite his not using the *term* anagram within that context. However, as difficult as it is to express to the reader what I believe Kant has been saying it is virtually impossible to do likewise with Hegel. On this topic Hegel is far too abstruse to be "said," he must instead literally be read in order to get a firm handle on what he is telling us.

One should understand that the anagram by its very definition possesses the "unconditioned completeness" required under Kant's theory. Unconditioned means something which is unaffected or influenced by one's opinions or naive sense of morality but, rather, is influenced by a full awareness of appropriate distinctions in thought. Under our conventional wisdom, an anagram is a new statement developed from an original statement, by simply transposing the letters in the original statement. I discovered through experimentation that the above application of anagrams, combined with an appropriate alphabetically based key and requisite contextual extensions lends the necessary and sufficient objective rigor resolving the issue of one's ability to review the kinds of examples to which Kant alluded.

Moreover, Kant is representing that his work is as complete an explanation of the knowledge as can be given. He makes this claim without his supplying, in any direct way, the conditions under which one can make the required discoveries that lead to the so- called "common principle." The simple principle that would completely uncover and expose the real meaning in regard to the substance of our discussion. And Kant is even suggesting his *Critique* is a model of the appropriate apparatus for the task. In other words, Kant is implying there is an inherent value in one's attempt and struggle to make the requisite discoveries. The *struggle* to apprehend is given as an essential of the knowledge itself. He states:

> For however completely all the *principles* of the system
> are presented in this *Critique*, the completeness of the
> system [his immediate system as well] itself *likewise* requires
> that none of the *derivative* concepts [the concepts which
> help evolve one's awareness of the existence of a key, and
> which can be derived solely from presupposition alone]

be lacking. [That is] These cannot be enumerated by any a priori computation, but must be *discovered* gradually. Whereas, therefore, in this *Critique* the entire *synthesis* of the concepts has been exhausted, there will still remain the further work of making their *analysis* [anagrammatic content analysis] similarly complete, a task which is rather an amusement [the process of developing a compendium of examples] than a labour. (Kant,1965, p.14)

I cannot say to what extent Kant is or is not correct in his implication of the value of what I refer to as "the struggle" involved in the learning process. I do know my protracted personal effort and active research to put this book together has indeed helped me discover the utility of the anagram to these matters. I might well have not discovered the value of anagrams without the struggle. It is an issue I am not prepared to reconcile at the moment. However, I might mention that in my personal experience I have always greatly benefited when individuals I asked helped to clarify ideas that were initially unclear.

According to Kant the "entire synthesis of the concepts" is there in his *Critique*. But we need more than just the synthesis of the concepts involved. In order to truly understand, we need to have examples that would serve to bring the concepts to life. Common sense suggests that in order for something to be labeled complete everything that relates to its composition must be represented there. And I completely understand that the developing of the "everything" cannot always be accomplished immediately, it can take some time. Kant even admits the effort required to study his text will not be complete, until his text along with its attendant concepts, in their entirety, are subjected to the "work," of what in my terms would be anagrammatic analysis. Consequently, I am obliged to agree with Kant. The expanded elements of a key are necessarily "discovered gradually," but in addition to the act of gradually expanding a key once it is discovered, my *emphasis* would be on those gradual discoveries of substantive facts which can only begin after one has discovered a key. Using a key developed from a common principle that would enable one to develop skills commensurate with the ability to cipher Kant's work is something that he tacitly appears to invite if not encourage. In other words, Kant believes the general system can be known completely and that he himself has written this complete system in the form and content of his *Critique*. That is, Kant appears to be of the opinion that his system is the complete theory, with respect to the kinds of concepts which can ultimately be derived regarding the topic under discussion, pure reason, albeit he acknowledges the obvious arrogance in these types of claims (ibid., p. 10). I must agree with Kant, his work is significant, with respect to his extensive outline of the theoretical underpinnings of knowledge and in terms of his style of presentation. His *Critique* is both unique and classic in that tradition. Kant appears content in having laid out a synthesis of the pertinent concepts, and then allowing time to mediate the balance of the work through the individual's struggle to understand the rest of what he is talking about. However there is no real assurance the individual can ever garner the necessary intellectual energy required to mediate to the final understanding of his work. The power of his work for me is how it gives credence to and support for the truths I had already discovered or rediscovered. That is, from the point of view that I had in earlier years read materials that made reference to Kant's work and doubtless those material offered me some partial insight into his theory. Although I had no way of knowing what was actually there to be comprehended and never imagined that I would eventually research and understand his work at the level I do now. Nevertheless, I will maintain the completeness of which he speaks is only a relative completeness. It falls on its face because he did not confide in his reader and provide his reader with any essential examples. Consequently, if clarity of understanding was truly his primary aim, the "entire synthesis" obviously cannot possibly be there. His work is missing the vital concept of the anagram. Although what synthesis he has given us is absolutely indispensable, his system lacks a single item of what he would call an example; and consequently, his system is incomplete. In other words, I must maintain the idea of incompleteness here, despite Kant's worthy contribution, for, with the use of anagrams, one immediately observes that the knowledge is in fact discovered gradually. Yet, and more importantly, one immediately becomes aware, upon introducing anagrams, that the substance of the information thus gathered increases constantly, and appears boundless with respect to its depth and breadth. I say this advisedly, because I now have the ability to look into the latent content, and my growth in learning has been none stop from the moment I acquired the above capability. In fact, I have ciphered a brief portion of Kant's table of contents, and I find there is a tremendous amount of substance there. Therefore, I can appreciate another sense in which Kant might have meant his is a complete work. His work does reveal some interesting content from the point of view of one's "sampling" his statements by means of a cipher. That is, from the point of view of ciphering only portions of his written work. For example, if we sample Kant's statement "the bright colouring [sic] of the illustrative material" (Kant,1965, p.13), we get the following anagram:

Us wait

thing u

[you] trait

. . .

the

right

color.

The Mind Factory

F [fuck]

lame,

ill

foe.

I have provided this example as an early illustration to help get the reader grounded in what I am discussing. However, after the shock effect has waned off, the reader should guard himself/herself against overreacting to the statement and reserve final judgement on the interpretation of the contextual meaning in the above anagram, until he/she has completed a review of the information and anagrams I have provided in chapter four.

No matter, Kant has done us a tremendous favor with the incredible effort he has put forward in his *Critique*. We are fortunate the *Critique* is already written and one need not redo what has been achieved so effectively. If one attempts to modernize Kant's exposition with examples and illustrations, on a *line items* basis, one would likely fall victim to precisely the difficulties Kant sought to avoid, that is, the attempt would likely create some excessively large written volume of work. A voluminous extract and exposition would likely result, if one did not observe that anagrams can be the "perfect" mode of examples. And a sampling of anagrams is typically sufficient to open up the content in segments or general excerpts of any written materials. However, since Kant's work exists, one can experience its content on a more intimate level given a contemporary revelation of the "objects"—"things-in-themselves" and related processes—of which he so comprehensively, eloquently, yet passionately spoke.

Let us be clear about what Kant means when he uses the term

critique. In his own words:

> I do not mean by this a critique of books and systems, but of the faculty of reason in general, in respect of all knowledge after which it may strive *independently* of all experience. (Kant, p. 9)

Kant is attempting to explain that one's ability to reason and puzzle through to understand things within the context of pure reason is not something that is formally or systematically taught. He is referring to the kind of knowledge born of presuppositions or pure concepts, by one's own common wits so to speak. And without the conscious benefit of anything directly gathered through experience. Where does this knowledge which is independent of all experience have its origin, where does it reside, and of what type is it? Kant tells us it is the type of knowledge that is called "self-knowledge" (ibid., p. 9). Of course, as was mentioned earlier in an endnote, self- knowledge has a more inclusive meaning than merely knowledge of one's self. Even for Kant, as the content and context of his *Critique* makes clear, his concept of self-knowledge does not refer simply and exclusively to knowledge of self, additionally, he is referring to the knowledge one teaches oneself by way of pure reasoning. Pure reasoning that is based on presuppositions, a priori knowing [Cogito ergo sum]. We can know this is what he meant because as he himself says:

> I have to deal with nothing save reason itself and its pure thinking; and to obtain complete knowledge of these, there is no need to go far afield, since I come upon them in my own self. Common logic itself supplies an example, how all the simple acts of reason can be enumerated [listed] completely and systematically. The subject [basis] of the present enquiry is the [kindred] question, how much we can hope to achieve by reason, when all the material and

assistance of experience are taken away. (ibid., pp. 10–11)

By "complete knowledge of these," Kant is referring to "reason" and "pure thinking" itself. Those things honed through original and personal mental experience, including the study of or reflection on general ideas, clever linguistic tricks, literary devices, and usable linguistic keys. When Kant speaks of "common logic," he is referring to common sense. The "taken away" of which he speaks is ultimately impossible. We cannot just arbitrarily erase what is embedded in our brains. Kant speaks on the "mind" devoid of all experience, but he is fully aware it is an "ideal" that can never actually be reached. We can only attempt to temporarily ignore or suspend what we already know. Thus Kant is also exploring the larger question of what man can create starting from scratch—that little or nothing, and that which exposes who we are within ourselves. This approach helps answer the question of where all learning comes from. The ultimate answer lies within man's predetermined perceived wisdom, which in fact is based on some direct prior mental experience. By the time we are matured enough to even consider the matter before us, we already have a storehouse of information embedded within us willy-nilly. It is quite simple, each generation of mankind has acquired and then learns some additional profound things during its time on this planet.

Then Kant made a statement that, in my mind, is the pivotal point upon which his *Critique* stands or falls. It is the representation of the fact that would establish his theory on the firm footing of an exact science. As he states it: Any knowledge that professes to hold a priori lays claim to be regarded as absolutely necessary.

This applies still more to any determination of all pure a priori knowledge, since such determination has to serve as the measure, and therefore as the [supreme] example (basis), of all apodeictic (philosophical) certainty. (parenthetical notes are my emphasis) (ibid., p. 11)

This is all much simpler than it initially sounds. In fact, what Kant is saying here is so obvious that to make it plain broaches on causing him to appear to be simplistic. Consequently it is important to emphasize that the point he is making is a very pivotal one. He is saying that all of the basic elements that are to be used for the creation of anything are "absolutely necessary" to the production of the thing. For example, if one wanted to make a cake, one would have to have all of the "ingredients" that are essential to the cake's production. Thus, in Kant's terms, the cake's ingredients are considered to be absolutely necessary. Since we have to start somewhere, the starting point is necessarily the measure of the real value and uniqueness of everything that develops from it. Consequently, if one wants to create a new language from scratch, one must begin with some initial symbols. Those first symbols then, in the above subtle sense, are considered to be absolutely necessary otherwise there could be no start up, there could be no beginning. What is actually being stated here is that a specific quantity of knowledge has to exist before an expanded knowledge base can take form and thus be made to appear for purposes of demonstration. The demonstration [determination in Kant's terms] establishes the certainty of the knowledge. Thus all knowledge has a prehistory. Kant further elucidates this pivotal idea by using a figurative Greek theorist as his example in stating:

> A new light flashed upon the mind of the first man (be he Thales or some other) who demonstrated the properties of the isosceles triangle. The true method, so he found, was not to inspect what he discerned either in the figure, or in the bare concept of it, and from this, as it were, to read off its properties; but, [rather,] to bring out what was necessarily implied in the concepts that he had himself formed a priori, and had put into the figure in the

construction by which he presented it to himself. If he is to know [or knows] anything with a priori certainty he must not ascribe to the figure anything save what necessarily follows from what he has himself set into it in accordance with his concept. (ibid., p. 19)

The idea here is that knowledge as we know it is a construction, for appearance and reproductive purposes, of an a *priori* [a prior "I" or "me" of an experience based] method of thinking . . . or thought life. He comes full circle with this idea when he continues in a more contemporary context by stating:

> A light broke upon all students of nature. They learned that reason has insight only into that which it produces after a plan of its own, and that it must not allow itself to be kept, as it were, in nature's leading-strings, but must itself show the way [evolve] with principles of judgement based upon fixed laws, constraining [forcing] nature to give answer to questions of reason's own determining. (ibid., p. 20)

This is a vital point, and we need not go much farther beyond this point in our effort to pull all the pieces together. Man creates, man constructs, and language is one of these ever-evolving constructions. In Kant's words:

> Accidental observations, made in obedience to no previously thought-out plan, can never be made to yield a necessary law, which alone reason I concerned to discover. Reason, holding in one hand its principles, according to which alone concordant appearances [that is, words which agree or work very well together] can be admitted as equivalent to laws, and in the other hand the experiment which it has devised in conformity with these principles,

must approach nature in order to be taught by it. It must not, however, do so in the character of a pupil who listens to everything that the teacher chooses to say, but of an appointed judge who compels the witnesses to answer questions which he has himself formulated . . . It is thus that the study of nature has entered on the secure path of a science, after having for so many centuries been nothing but a process of merely random groping. (ibid., pp. 20–21)

In the sense that his work "compels the witnesses to answer questions," Kant's work is truly groundbreaking. I emphasized and suggested earlier that Kant would have reason through a *priori* knowledge to create and *then* to construct objects. Our everyday *words* are the primary objects in Kant's intellectual field. He observes:

As regards objects which are thought solely through reason, and indeed as necessary, but which can never—at least not in the manner in which reason thinks them—be given in experience, the attempts at thinking them (for they must admit of being thought) will furnish an excellent touchstone of what we are adopting as our new method of thought, namely, that we can know a priori of things only what we ourselves put into them [the words]. (ibid., p. 23)

Kant obviously does not have much confidence that many people could think through to seeing inside his proposed method of thought. However, he implies any successful "attempts" would necessarily exhibit the requisite criterion of having to rely on one's personal knowledge to achieve this end.

On this point, before continuing with Kant's delineation of his theory, I should take the time to make sure the reader is completely in touch with and understanding precisely what is being discussed.

When Kant refers to "objects" and to "things" in the last quote, he is using the terms synonymously. The thing or object, in the one sense in which he is using meaning here, is that which we recognize in our everyday understanding as a common word. Words that are contained within a word are one of the senses of the notion Kant is referring to when he introduces the concept of "things-in- themselves." After the reader has had the opportunity to read chapter 4, he/she will have an even clearer notion of what the "things-in-themselves" are by way of this initial characterization, but first we need review some additional foundational information.

Earlier, I had discussed the concepts of manifest and latent content. Every word has both a manifest and a still larger latent content. By the manifest content of a given word, I am referring here to the conventional everyday denotative and connotative meanings in regard to word content, which is the dictionary and experientially based assignment of meanings as word content. The manifest content or meaning is merely the apparent word content. It is what the words appear to mean. This is the context in which Kant uses the term "appearance." On the other hand, the latent content being referred to here is a content issuing from reading a cipher. And it is more than mere double entendre. The latent content is a wider substance and is typically contrary to the manifest content. The cipher is a reduction of a given word or phrase into another and different word or phrase. It reduces the word to the elements that potentially created it, and where the elements have pre-assigned meanings. Yet there is no conflict, both levels of content are equally legitimate, in the sense of possessing meanings relevant in our everyday world and in our everyday life. Language is constructed in the above way, and for the purpose of storing information, as well as, communicating information. Latent content primarily performs the above storage function, while manifest content performs the communication function.

The following diagram introduces some additional critical insight. It is insight I feel is essential for the readers to grasp for the purpose of loosening up their typically conventional rigid notion of what a word really is.

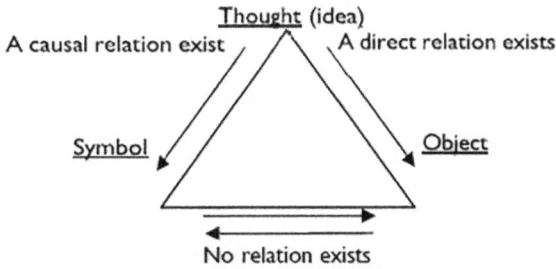

In their classic and seminal work, *The Meaning of Meaning*, Ogden and Richards (1923) point out the absolute distinction that must be made between the *thought*, the *object*, and the *symbol* used within the context of language, thought, and action. More specifically, they point out that while there is a "direct" relation between the thought and the object, a causal relation between the thought and the symbol, there is however no "relevant" relation that exists between an object and its *symbol* (ibid., p. 11). This idea has a dual meaning. On the one hand, the symbols of the object word or phrase are the letters that constitute the word or phrase. On the other hand, there is the distinction to be made between the physical object and the whole word that symbolizes the physical object. For example, there is absolutely no relevant relation existing between the word "chair" and the object we habitually associate with it. Within this context, the fact that there is a causal relation between the thought and the object is significant for us. An anagram is a manipulation of the symbols or letters of the object word or phrase. The manipulation of the "symbols" prior to their introduction and purpose for use in a predetermined combination as a word or phrase necessarily defines a causal relation between the thought and the object word, and the process is properly labeled encryption. The manipulation in the opposite direction of the symbols or letters of a given word or phrase, at some point after the fact of a word's or phrase's creation, for the purpose of deciphering the previously encrypted meaning in the word or phrase I refer to as its cipher. The cipher is the discovery of at least "a" logical content, and not necessarily "the" logical content, of what one presupposes has been encrypted. We cannot "know" the content in an absolute or final objective sense, because there is no limit to the number of possible keys that can determine a content. However, one can develop a meaningful and useful logical content consistent with any appropriately predetermined key, which is based on a presupposed universe of discourse. The process is embedded in the very character of the lexicon. Keep in mind that I am only reducing conventional language in the present text, and using a single key to that purpose.

In this regard, all forms of "conventional language" fall within my purview, and that includes the formal and informal forms of a variety of languages, phonics, slang, colloquialisms, and even invectives [curse words]. Moreover, all of the above forms of language are useful and relevant within this context. In this regard, you are to consider this variety of linguistic elements special weapons and tactics, in the war to establish greater clarity of understanding the issues of life.

I could use a specific word here as an illustration, but I have chosen to use the title of the Kant text being discussed, because its use will be much more illustrative of the point to be made. The one thing that should be most obvious to the reader and that he/she will be obliged to bear witness to is, I could not possibly have had a priori or prior knowledge of what Kant wrote, because Kant's text predates my writings by more than two hundred years. The following example is an anagrammatic reduction of the above title and is based on a specific key. I will first express it to you in piece-meal fashion.

Pure Reason

Person

u[you]

are

Notice the statement below the underlined phrase is made up exclusively of the letters in the original phrase.

Critique of

c[see] wit

I.Q. of

u[you]

e[he]

We can now observe a meaningful content associated with the complete title.

Critique of Pure Reason

c[see]

wit I.Q.

of

person

The Mind Factory

u[you]

are

u[you]

e[he] (= mc²)

What is being expressed in the statement of this anagram is consistent with Kant's definition of "self-knowledge." By Kant's own description, one only comes to an understanding of the "things-in- themselves" after achieving self-knowledge. I interpret the above cipher to mean that what more we are able to learn, after a given moment in time, is very much dependent on what we already know about ourselves and what we already know in general. And it lays specific emphasis on the knowledge content obtained from the cryptic wit or information inherent in a cipher. Any personal interpretation of data is informed by information we have personally read and experienced, both directly and vicariously. In contrast to Kant's appellation of self-knowledge, I refer to this level of knowing as personal knowledge. However, he and I are likely to be meaning the same thing. Again, I have provided a large group of anagrams of this type for the reader to review in the next chapter. In the interim, however, we need to continue following Kant's exposition for there is still more we should uncover to complete our understanding.

PART TWO

As we continue following Kant's dialogue, the best way to bring out the depth and breadth of his comments is to remain consistent with my inserting commentary into some of the quotes we attribute to him as well as summarize their contents. At least then, the uninitiated will be able to readily follow what I am claiming Kant's words mean with an immediate clarity.

First of all, we should understand Kant was attempting to reconcile what initially would appear to be a very curious opinion. It is the notion that for the most part everything there is to know about reason and pure thinking in regard to all possible human experience is already known. He was thus interested in making a contribution to establishing whether or not any more could be known, and doing so using scientifically established procedures and theory. He believed science had previously reached the limits or boundaries of all possible experience. That means he was of the opinion that science had discovered all there was to discover, with respect to the fundamentals of knowledge about human nature and had delineated or distributed all it had discovered, through direct or vicarious real experience, within the medium we call language. The activity of finding and storing knowledge within the confines of language is what he considered is the purpose and method of science. Still, he was desirous of exploring the possibility of and the theoretical potential for somehow breaking new intellectual ground. As Kant observes:

> We are brought to the conclusion that we can never transcend the limits of possible experience, though that is precisely what this science [it was known then as metaphysics] is concerned, above all else, to achieve. (ibid., p. 24)

Of course, as mortal beings, we can never personally experience all there is to experience. However, the theory is that as members of society we can experience everything, if not directly at least vicariously, since all those findings are recorded in the words and the concepts of language. And Kant believed historical science had indeed already completed the job. At least for him, one would have to prove the converse, that science had not yet completed the job. As such, once we discover the purpose and method of science, we are necessarily left with the impression that everything we might create intellectually has already been created, despite the fact that most of us are still just discovering the creative method as it exists in language construction. The limits of experience, in other words, deals with anticipated actions or actual experience, and having them both be well-defined and, where necessary, be recorded even before they have ever occurred, immediately upon their being thought of as a real time possibility. Of course, actual experience would be recorded upon its being determined to be naturally immutable. He further suggests that:

> This situation yields, however, just the very experiment by which, indirectly, we are enabled to prove the truth of this first estimate of our a *priori* knowledge of reason [what mankind has thought about, created, and could possibly create], namely that such knowledge has to do only with appearances [whole words themselves], and must leave the thing in itself [the ciphered word] as indeed real *per* se, but as not known to us [at least should not be acknowledged by us]. For what necessarily forces us to transcend the limits of experience and of all appearances is the *unconditioned*, which reason, by necessity and by right [the right here refers to eminent domain . . . that is since the power and ability to design things in this special way existed—in the hands of others—before we came into existence], demands in things in themselves (people), as required to complete the series [list] of conditions. (ibid.)

By the "limits of experience," we should understand Kant means all established facts and all actions with at least the potential of becoming established facts that have ever been known or could within limits become known to mankind. The substance of these two kinds of facts, also referred to as "empirical knowledge," is encrypted within the composition of words and becomes the substance of what we call language, i.e., language is composed of encrypted words. A given word is being referred to as an "appearance." We do not initially recognize that they are encrypted, yet the manifest contents of words are only a facade of what they actually represent. What he means by the "unconditioned" then is one's intellectual *perspective*, once one recognizes and accepts the distinction between "appearance" and the "limits of experience" (ibid.). That is, the expression "unconditioned" is tacitly being contrasted with the "conditioned." One who merely knows what there is to be known about words as manifest content or appearance, and yet knows nothing about how appearance is created by latent content as the limits of experience, is among those who are considered the "conditioned." Now then what more can be said about real or empirical knowledge—the limits of experience—as opposed to simple appearance? Kant says the following:

> If, then, on the supposition that our empirical knowledge conforms to objects as things in themselves, we find that the unconditioned cannot be *thought without contradiction*, and that when, on the other hand, we suppose that our representation of things, as they are given to us, does not conform to these things as they are in themselves, but that these objects, as appearances, conform to our mode of representation, the *contradiction vanishes*. (ibid.)

In other words, and the logic here is mere common sense, if no distinction is to be made between appearance and empirical knowledge as the limits of experience one would not be able to imagine the unconditioned, and thus thoughts could be discussed without unveiling contradiction. On the other hand, if we are able to see things in their unconditioned nature, we cannot avoid coming face to face with contradiction. By its very definition, unconditioned thought brings opposition and contrariness into our awareness and understanding. For example, the very introduction of the refined distinction between the notion of manifest content and the opposing latent content is unconditioned thought.

The question remains, for the newcomer to these discoveries, whether or not everything has already been said, or whether there is any room to go beyond what has already been given as the outer limits of possible experience? Certainly nothing precludes our inquiring in this regard. Kant himself says;

> It is still open to us to enquire whether, in the practical knowledge of reason [what is popular wisdom in Freud's terms], data may not [yet] be found sufficient to determine reason's transcendent [subsequent or next] concept of the unconditioned, and so to enable us, in accordance with the wish of metaphysics, and by means of knowledge that is possible a priori, though only from a practical point of view, to pass beyond the limits [because our thoughts and man- kinds living history as it relates to the popular wisdom is already contained in existing words and concepts of language—and were known before we were conscious of them, it seems virtually impossible for the nascent individual to go beyond the extant limits] of all possible experience. [ibid., pp. 24–25]

This issue of whether "data may not be found" also refers to what Kant suggests is the "experiment of *reduction*." (ibid., p. 24) This experimental technique is what we know in modern terms as reductionism. Reductionism, within this context, is the process of breaking down the objects under discussion, even considering the manifold of their meanings, into "their most elementary forms" as things-in-themselves. I am proposing using anagrams as an appropriate reduction technique. However, we certainly will not discover anything that is not already in the objects regardless of what key one may use.

The science and application of reduction techniques, which are based on established principles, is what Kant refers to as "metaphysics" (ibid., p. 68). He says this of metaphysics:

> Metaphysics has to deal only with principles [people], and with the limits of their employment [literally] as determined by these principles [people] themselves, and it [metaphysics] can therefore finish its work and bequeath to posterity as a capital [good] to which no addition can be made. Since it is a fundamental science, it is under obligation to achieve this completeness. (ibid., p. 26)

Kant wants to establish for himself that the fundamental system of language construction is complete. He is seeking control of the system so he can have confidence or even be assured that no one and nothing can alter it. His reaction seems a bit odd, but he explains his point of view when he says:

> These principles [people] properly belong [not to reason—or secular and practical thought—but] to sensibility [the spiritual and the speculative realm], and when thus employed they threaten to make the bounds of sensibility coextensive with the real, and so to supplant reason in its pure (practical) employment. So far, therefore, as our Critique limits speculative reason, it is indeed *negative*; but since it thereby removes an obstacle which stands in the way of the employment of practical reason, nay threatens to destroy it [any obstacle to practical reason], it has in reality a *positive* and very important use. (ibid., p. 26)

94

Kant obviously has some serious concerns about how people think. In other words, in his opinion the thought life of people needs to be controlled. He is unequivocal in the statement of his intent to limit speculative reasoning. In his mind, speculative reasoning is the mechanism that would potentially open our universe of discourse to undesirable changes and even cause the destruction of the system as originally designed. Moreover, he states:

> Though we cannot know these objects as things in themselves, we must yet be in position at least to *think* them as things in themselves; otherwise we should be landed in the absurd conclusion that there can be appearance without anything that appears. (ibid., p. 27)

The "we" he is referring to could be the "we" who are to arrive on his intellectual level. Of course, an earlier anagram suggested those he expected to arrive at his intellectual level would be assisted, if they possessed the correct "trait." There is an obvious tension running through his writings here. Perhaps there is even a double entendre?! It sounds as if he wants it both ways but he cannot have it both ways. It is as if Kant is saying "those who know don't tell, those who tell don't know." He does not appear to be facing up to the fact it is impossible to conceal these matters from public view. He is in denial because he has made the naïve assumption others outside his well-defined cabal did not, could not, and should not know these matters intricately. As far as Kant is concerned then, we should be free to know and think that things-in- themselves do exist. However, it appears he would argue that other than members of his cabal, people should not be permitted to speculate about or to closely examine the specific objects in an effort to know what internally exists within the objects of our attention when they are viewed as things-in-themselves. He is not comfortable with the idea of people having the means of actually knowing what is going on behind the scenes, so to speak. Yet he would always want members of his cabal to be in a "position" to observe, clandestinely, and to possess the skills to evaluate even *moderate* what would be going on behind the scenes.

I appreciate the fact that Kant shows a strategic willingness to allow into his way of thinking the possibility of one at least "thinking" of the object words as things-in-themselves. That is, he is willing to at least stipulate that something is in fact going on behind the scenes. For in actuality, the inability to comfortably and routinely think of the object words fundamentally as things-in-themselves— thus being constrained to always experience or sense "appearance without anything that appears"—is the stuff minimally of mental illness, even madness. Consequently, my work is an obvious departure from what Kant sought to do. I personally have no problem with speculative reasoning and the potential for change issuing from it, where everyday people are forced to become better informed, and are additionally empowered to better use their common sense. Change is a social fact! Therefore I have no concern about people becoming aware things are happening behind the scenes; and, more importantly, I have only a marginal concern that everyday people can know some of what is *actually* going on behind the scenes. Many ordinary people already do understand these matters, and I am under the strong impression that society can only benefit from more people understanding these things.

What the issue really is all about can be captured in the following statement, which represents a footnote in Kant's *Critique*:

> To *know* an object, I must be able to prove its possibility, either from its actuality as attested by experience, or a *priori* by means of reason. But I can *think* whatever I please, provided only that I do not contradict myself, that is, provided my concept is a possible thought. This suffices for the possibility of the concept, even though I

may not be able to answer for there being, in the sum of all possibilities, an object corresponding to it [that is, even though I may not know which particular one of a range of physical object choices, at an instance, would be the best one to use to represent the "appearance" for the concept]. But something more is required before I can ascribe to such a concept objective validity, that is, real possibility; the former possibility is merely logical. This something more need not, however, be sought in the theoretical sources of knowledge; it may lie in those that are practical (ibid.).

First of all, recall Kant is subtly expressing his doubt that people can prove the possibility of a pervasive and consistent latent content in objects. Secondly, he is suggesting and encouraging us, in the event one does discover what is "possible" in regard to objects, to conduct oneself and one's actions in a certain way. In fact, Kant is lecturing and/or cautioning any persons whom would be lucky enough to find himself/herself in a position to engage in language construction about what he/she should or should not do in that regard. And his above comments now make it clear that he has concluded it is possible to extend the limits of all possible experience. Because he is saying one should be sure when constructing or creating any single new appearances, neologisms if you will, beyond the extant limits of possible experience to be certain the new objects also have real possibility in practical terms. In other words, one should not just throw something into the mix without supplying the requisite practical use for it. He insists that any new concept that is assigned a symbol should be associated with a real physical object that has a practical use, and its construction should fit within the continuity of the lexicon. But Kant is troubled by the thought of more than a select group of individuals being involved in the activity of word construction. So he is suggesting that within the extant universe of discourse, there does occur a more routine and ordinary activity for the ordinary scholar to consider, formal analysis.

Kant is hinting one need not concern oneself with the intricate inner workings of word construction because there is an equally interesting and related body of work one could involve oneself with in lieu of latent content analysis. It is the kind of work most theorists do anyway. As Kant informs us:

> What keeps us, during the actual building, free from all apprehension and suspicion, and flatters us with a seeming thoroughness, is this other circumstance, namely, that a great, perhaps the greatest, part of the business of our reason consists in analysis of the concepts which we already have as objects. This analysis supplies us with a considerable body of knowledge, which, while nothing but explanation or elucidation of what has already been thought in our concepts, though in a confused manner, is yet prized as being, at least as regards its form, new insight. But so far as the matter or content is concerned, there has been no extension of our previously possessed concepts, but only an analysis of them. (ibid., p. 47)

Of course, nothing precludes our analysis of both the uncovered latent and the given manifest contents as contents. Anagrams and sensibility can help facilitate the analysis of latent contents. Common sense and formal logic can help facilitate the analysis of manifest contents. It is obvious one's involvement in the standard, traditional approaches to the analysis of extant materials relative to their manifest contents offer no concern for Kant. It is the unlimited types of analyses that could potentially be generated from pure thought that troubles him. Therefore he expresses his desire that we be sure to be clear in our own minds that we know what we are advocating. In that effort, he proposes that we have a well thought out "doctrine" that defines the parameters of our potential excursions into the study of knowledge. He suggests that:

If we are to make a systematic division of the science which we are engaged in presenting, it must have first a doctrine of the elements, and secondly, a *doctrine of the method* of pure reason. . . . By way of introduction or anticipation we need only say that there are two stems of human knowledge, namely, *sensibility* and *understanding*, which perhaps spring from a common, but to us unknown, root. Through the former, objects are given to us; through the latter, they are thought [in the above sense of conventional, formal analysis]. Now in so far as sensibility may be found to contain a priori representations constituting the condition under which objects are given to us, it will belong to transcendental philosophy. (ibid., pp. 61–62)

At this point we appear to have a double entendre. It is my impression that Kant is using the rubric of transcendental philosophy in a dual sense with regard to the idea of sensibility. The one sense is that any discussions about sensibility should remain on an *esoteric* level, that is, any information about the concept of sensibility should remain limited to a very select few. In the other sense, sensibility is to be viewed in its ethereal or otherworldly character where we simply acknowledge and emphasize our total inability to completely know the true wellspring or source of our sensibility. At one point, Kant gives us an adequate definition of the notion of intuition, and there he locates intuition within our sensibility (ibid., pp. 65–66). In using the term *intuition*, I am content to have us rely on our conventional understanding and everyday usage of the term's meaning. Of course, sensibility is to be interpreted as "sense ability." The heightened ability to sense what is occurring in one's immediate environment. The following series of two related diagrams should mentally assist you in understanding the flow of what is being discussed above:

B. sensuous (spirit)

A. <u>Things-in-themselves</u>

<u>Semiotics</u>
(objects/word and their anagrams)

<u>sexual</u> (secular)

B. <u>sensuous</u> (spirit)

<u>sensibility</u> (secular)
(spiritual and speculative)

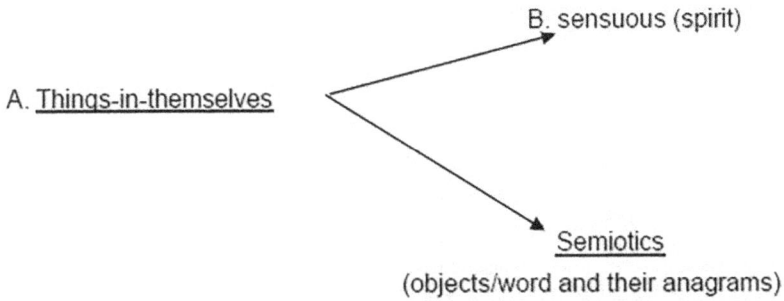

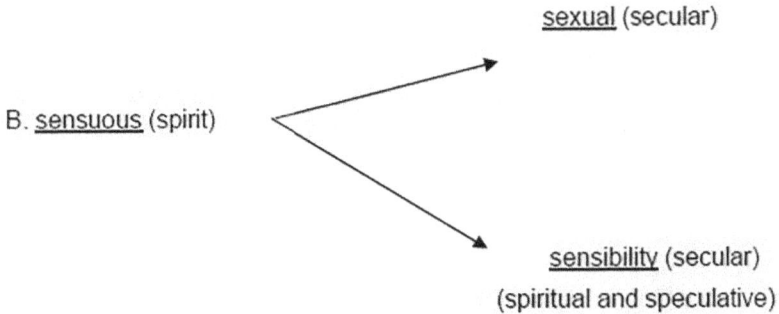

The next statement has given me pause and cause to doubt Kant could have supplied us with examples appropriate to our discussion. He expresses his own doubt when he states:

> Even if we could bring our intuition to the highest degree of clearness, we should not thereby come any nearer to the constitution [composition] of objects in themselves. We should [Or does he mean "would" . . . ?] still know only our [personal] mode of intuition, that is, our [subjective] sensibility. . . . What the objects may be in themselves would never become known to us even through the most enlightened knowledge of that which is alone given us, namely, their appearance. . . . For the difference between

a confused and a clear representation is merely logical [the correct context must be found], and does not concern the content. No doubt the concept of "right," in its common-sense usage, contains all that the subtlest speculation can develop out of it, though in its ordinary and practical use we are not conscious of the manifold [many and various] representations comprised in this thought. But we cannot say that the common concept is therefore sensible, containing mere appearance.

For "right" can never be [only] an appearance; it is a concept in the understanding, and represents a property (the moral property) of actions, which belongs to them [who—intellectually—are those who see things as they are not, as they want them to be, or feel they somehow ought to be] in themselves. (ibid., p. 83)

The word "should" is pivotal to our understanding the nuance of his meaning in the above quote. Does he mean "would" instead of should? Or is he perhaps again suggesting we should not reveal the other side of what fully represents our sensibility, once sensibility has been achieved? He might even be using a Socratic approach to explanation here. It would be difficult to discern which it is. As brilliant as Kant's writings are, he sometimes reminds me of some of the intellectually and emotionally challenged individuals who appear as students in some of my courses. It should be obvious to all that we can never achieve the elusive objective absolute on this level of knowledge. That absolute certainly does not exist for us as students of the medium. The very best we can do is offer our subjective interpretations within an objective context. In this regard, as I mentioned earlier, and Hegel bears witness to it, when viewed as a proof, each anagram serves us well. There is a reason why we cannot know about all things absolutely. Only God possesses that ability. However, it is difficult to convince the unbeliever that these are all elements of God's wisdom, and we cannot ever possibly know everything or know anything with the exactitude or precision to which God knows it, although it is God's desire that we understand what his wisdom entails (Pro. 4:7).

At any rate, it is time we review and experience some examples of what these first three chapters have been leading up to . . . an arbitrary but well-defined sampling of anagrams. In other words and unlike Kant, I am willing to provide some examples; and, after all that has been said, not to be concerned that people are yet so obtuse they will not be able to appreciate what they will be seeing.

In doing so, I propose I will have unequivocally taken my readers deeper into the theory than any other modern-day writer writing about formal sociological theory has taken them.

CHAPTER FOUR

HOW DO WE KNOW? (PART ONE)

Let no man deceive himself. If any man among you seemeth to be wise in this world, let him become a fool, that he may be wise.
—1 Cor. 3:18

As was intended, this chapter has turned out to be the centerpiece of my book. The chapter has two main purposes: one is to convince the reader, by way of an incontestable and undeniable demonstration of "examples," which I believe are of a type on par with anything Immanuel Kant *could* have developed that all literary forms possess a latent intellectual content. The other is to reveal a sufficiently diverse content within the given examples necessary to provide the reader with some additional everyday information perhaps not previously known. The importance of the latter purpose is that it permits the reader to develop a natural appreciation for the value of the latent content of literary forms, over and above their manifest contents. Additionally, the substance of this chapter is my way of assisting the reader in the self-development of the skill of ciphering. In this regard, it is essential that each element of this initial group of examples actually be read as a whole if not in the given order. The content of some of the derivations in the earlier anagrams will assist the reader in understanding the other remaining anagrams, and ultimately will provide the reader, given the benefit of the key I have provided, with the wherewithal to develop anagrammatic interpretations on his/her own. This conceptual foundation will even assist the reader in "expanding" or growing the original key. The key I have given is a "seed" of its greater self and is necessary and sufficient to the *random* set of anagrams I have provided, together with the technical application and development of the concept of anagram, which is simply transposition of the original letters. It is important to emphasize that the key I have provided is both a *neutral* key and it is only part of itself. I mean the key is neutral in the sense that I have deliberately avoided use of any key that would have revealed a more highly controversial political content. For if clearly understood, what has been revealed in the given anagrams is controversial enough. The key is not only neutral in the above sense but it is also a "universal" key. That is, anything which I would refer to within this context as a "key" can be applied in *all languages* concurrently and, as given, without alteration yet revealing a meaningful content. A "key" can be applied to the major part of the native script of any language. The key given below is a seed of the larger key which can be *grown* from itself in an ever "expanding universe" of discourse. In addition, there still exists a potentially limitless set of other distinct keys or seeds of keys, if you will, which are not as neutral with respect to revealed content. I have provided the given key because one needs somewhere to begin in this knowledge. The key I have supplied is to serve as a starter kit. The key affirms its own existence, and its existence will help to keep those who traverse this intellectual terrain well grounded. With respect to the given examples, I initially continuously use the key, until I am confident the reader has had enough time and direct exposure to understand the application. However, after a point, in some instances I simply supply the words in the reduction of the anagram. In doing so, I have to assume that the reader by then has understood that the words in the anagrams are based on the key. Of course, as I have already suggested, none of the anagrams I have developed are limited to the anagrammatic interpretations I have supplied. More specifically, other and different anagrammatic interpretations potentially exist for the same word and phrases I originally used and even using the same key or sub-key.

As had been mentioned earlier, and regardless of whether or not the reader initially chooses to accept and believe it, the ability to grow a key very much depends on the guidance given by the Holy Spirit. Additionally, in the most essential ways, it is also dependent on the reader's "self-knowledge" or "personal knowledge," as the reader would subjectively understand or prefer the concept. These two related and overlapping concepts are not easily ratcheted down. The reader should use his/her own subjective judgement or understanding to choose which of the two terms is the more "inclusive" expression of the concept. That is, if the reader's understanding of the concept of self-knowledge would exhaust all of Polanyi's points yet still not be limited to what Michael Polanyi (1962) refers to as personal knowledge, then self-knowledge is what I mean. If, on the other hand, the reader's individual definition of the idea of personal knowledge exhausts and yet has a content bigger and more inclusive than Polanyi's definition, then personal knowledge is what is to be understood in this connection. I choose to use personal-knowledge as my meaning here only because I feel comfortable with the concept, without further defining the concept. Albeit I do so with the understanding that each one of us has some "sense" of what can be meant by either concept. Again, by this I mean any and all knowledge known by me personally or relating in any way whatsoever to myself or to my personal experiences alone. Moreover, as by my own definition and understanding, I can only know a portion of what I refer to as my personal-knowledge. As was mentioned much earlier, only the Holy Spirit, an entity greater than myself, can know my individual personal-knowledge perfectly and completely.

We are typically given to thinking the concept of an anagram is an occasional entertaining diversion. That is correct! Developing anagrams is an entertaining diversion. The process is also "an amusement" in the sense in which Kant has expressed the notion (Kant, 1965, p. 14). However, one must come to appreciate it as much more than that. It is a method used to sample and explore the secret and the extraordinary embedded as the latent content of literary materials, thus all written and oral linguistic materials.

We must allow ourselves to let the anagrams be read and treated like poetry. I say like poetry because one must use one's personal-knowledge to provide the interpretation appropriate to one's own consciousness level; or, rather, one's personal level of experience based understanding. The reality of the situation is simple! The more one understands the more one will be able to understand. The more one knows the more one can be prepared to know. As a result of their character, the meanings in some anagrams I have supplied will necessarily appear equivocal to the examiner while others will be unequivocal. Each individual anagram possesses an infinite malleability based on the potential diversity of keys and the multiple possible transpositions on any given set of letters. Therefore there is no shorter way to present the anagrams for examination, other than allowing for the freedom of interpretation similar to what is inherent in poetic interpretation. In this sense, as a concept, what I refer to as an anagram is consistent with what the renowned sociologist Emile Durkheim (1966) refers to as "epigram," and the definition of an epigram does emphasize the poetic element (ibid., p. 46). As I see it, any other approach would require our getting bogged down in unmanageable extended explanations, which themselves could only be based on someone's subjective judgement. It would necessitate our writing volumes of materials, which is precisely the situation Kant mentioned he sought to avoid. In allowing for various interpretations, we permit the anagrams to objectively speak for themselves, as determined by context and based on the previously determined key assignment. No matter, this should not offer us any serious concern. In fact, it is the desired outcome. As in the case of the definition of words, it is the multiple diverse usages and interpretations in context which gives them their fullness. This fact would ultimately be true in the case of anagrams were they manageable enough to be listed like word definitions in a dictionary. However, the character or nature of an anagram would require we develop a separate dictionary for each different key assignment.

There is a definite correlation between the way in which I understand and explain these ideas in relation to anagrams and the sociological discourse of Emile Durkheim. I have been discussing the value of studying the Bible and anagrams for the purpose of understanding the popular wisdom. Emile Durkheim (ibid.) uses the analogous concepts of "the proverbs and epigrams," which leads me to believe, if Durkheim and I are not saying the exact same thing, we are definitely saying something very similar. In his words:

> To achieve an understanding of customs and popular beliefs, one must investigate the proverbs and epigrams that express them (ibid., p.46).

The anagrams I am supplying as examples have been culled from a larger original set and set aside for this publication. Still, I have had to provide a sufficiently large number of them so the necessary impact of the overall range of content is imparted. Again, this is done with the purpose of eliminating any doubt whatsoever that anagrams yield a bountiful latent content. Additionally, the random sampling of diverse literary material is used to demonstrate that anagrams can be "reduced" from any literary forms, and our sampling is an objective one. Moreover, once established, the key gives the intuitive or introspective interpretations that help to inform an anagram, based on one's storehouse of personal-knowledge, an impersonal rigor. That is, one cannot know upon first sight precisely what an anagram will reveal. Yet the anagram one creates is determined a priori as effected by the given key. However, from the point of view of developing an anagram, this still means its content is objectively determined. Since the statements to be "sampled" and analyzed are randomly selected and are based on a pre-established key, there are no early opportunities for one's "preconceptions" to taint a given anagram. The content of the anagrams are thus established rigorously (ibid., p. 31).

In the last chapter we reviewed what Immanuel Kant defined as "things-in-themselves," and developed the singular notion of a thing as being a word. Therefore, we saw the anagram represented, within context, the thing-in-itself. That is, finding the words that are embedded inside of words. In his seminal work, *The Rules of the Sociological Method*, Emile Durkheim (ibid.) succeeded in extending the general understanding and thus appreciation of what a word considered as a thing truly means.

Under Durkheim's consideration, being a "system of signs" language is a "social fact" (ibid., p. 2). He then argues that we are to "consider social facts as things" (ibid., p. 14). Thus again we see, among other uses, "things" being defined literally as the actual words of language. Durkheim provides us with his definition of a social fact, when he says:

> Here, then, is a category of facts with very distinctive characteristics: it consists of ways of acting, thinking, and feeling, external to the individual, and endowed with a power of coercion, by reason of which they control him (ibid., p. 3).

Society is "external to the individual" in the sense mentioned earlier. Society existed before the individual was born and thus the individual is constrained to conform to society's standards and not the other way around. This is Durkheim's meaning in the expression the "power of coercion. For example, we should understand that society and the individuals within it could not exist, much less function without some form of language or system of signs. Hence language can be said to possess coercive power over us. Any attempts to exist without a language would demonstrate the legitimacy of the point he is making.

If we accept Durkheim's definition, and we certainly should, words, names, and all other types of written forms of expression are social facts and thus things, in agreement with the Kantian sense of the notion. Moreover, in addition to the ways in which Durkheim defines a social fact, we need to appreciate a social fact as anything which mankind has had a hand in creating or augmenting, and possesses the coercive necessity mentioned, including language itself. What also needs to be noted is that despite the above agreement between Kant and Durkheim on what a thing is, Durkheim brings a profound subtlety of meaning with his definitive interpretation of the significance of this finding for sociology. Since language is a social fact and can be treated as a thing, language itself becomes data prime for sociological study. Then, as if to say the above observation means little when compared to the specifics of what is to be studied within language, Durkheim says:

> Man cannot live in an environment without forming some ideas about it according to which he regulates his behavior. But because these ideas are nearer to us and more within our mental reach than the realities to which they correspond, we tend naturally to substitute them for the latter and to make them the very subject of our speculations. Instead of observing, describing, and comparing things, we are content to focus our consciousness upon, to analyze, and to combine our ideas.

> Instead of a science concerned with realities, we produce no more than an ideological analysis. (ibid., p. 14)

According to Durkheim many of our theories substitute our *ideas* of reality for actual reality, and we then make this detached set of ideas the subject of our discussions about reality. And, as was noted earlier, this is the same point that Kant made (Kant, 1965, p. 47). We do this in lieu of observing, describing, and explaining actual reality. Durkheim calls this habit "ideological analysis." Moreover, Durkheim is not impressed with the volumes of materials issuing from this habit of mind. C. Wright Mills (1959) might refer to this type of theorizing as "grand theory." The popular wisdom would likely see it as "grandstanding," an exhibition of the grandiose. As for Durkheim, while he does not mention Immanuel Kant by name on this point, Kant's *Critique* itself would likely be subsumed under the category of ideological analysis, because Durkheim calls the "transcendental insight" stuff "tyrannical" and "trifling" (Durkheim, 1966, pp. 32–34). With regard to how these theories sometimes posture themselves, I can appreciate Durkheim's sentiments and can totally agree with him on a practical level. However, even if Durkheim was including Kant's work in his criticism that discussion need not concern the present-day student on these matters, since what we are developing is, for all intents and purposes, a new tool for the analysis of all literary materials. Consequently, even that which is said to be trifling and tyrannical can yield information for us. In fact, often, there are significant revelations to be uncovered. Durkheim actually agrees with the point despite his criticisms and arguing from the point of view of a sociologist, Durkheim gives us more insight into his interpretation of these matters when he states that:

> In spite of all these doctrines, social phenomena are things and ought to be treated as things. To demonstrate this proposition, it is unnecessary to philosophize on their nature and to discuss the analogies they present with the phenomena of lower realms of existence. It is sufficient to note that they are the unique data of the sociologist. All that is given, all that is subject to observation, has thereby the character of a thing. To treat phenomena as things is to treat them as data, and these constitute the point of departure of science. Now social phenomena present this character incontestably. What is given is not the idea that men form of value, for that is inaccessible, but only the

values established in the course of economic relations; not conceptions of the moral ideal, but the totality of rules which actually determine conduct; not the idea of utility or wealth, but all the details of economic organization. Even assuming the possibility that social life is merely the development of certain ideas, these ideas are nevertheless not immediately given. They cannot be perceived or known directly, but only through the phenomenal reality expressing them. We do not know a priori whether ideas form the basis of the diverse currents of social life, nor what they are. Only after having traced these currents back to their sources shall we know whence they issue (ibid., pp. 27–28).

These comments indicate Durkheim is, willy-nilly, in agreement with my suggestion for contemporary students of knowledge. Since "these doctrines" so-called are social facts as written form, they are data and thus become ripe for study. Continuing with an important subtle point, Durkheim would have us clearly understand it is not what we think but what we actually do that matters with respect to the data sociologists should assign themselves to study and analyze. He is not referring to studying ideas merely as thoughts in the mind. Durkheim has concluded that ideas cannot possibly truly be known except through the observation of the way in which they are physically or empirically actualized. He further suggests that:

We must, therefore, consider social phenomena in themselves as distinct from the consciously formed representations of them in the mind; we must study them objectively as external things, for it is this character that they present to us (ibid., p. 28). Ideas can never appear to us as themselves. Ideas are akin to what the Spirit is, if not a form of Spirit themselves. We cannot see Spirit, and similarly we cannot see an idea. This is the primary sense in which meaning can be taken as manifest content from the following biblical verse:

So that things which are seen were not made of things which do appear (Heb. 11:3).

Hence there is another sense, within this context, in which we are using the terms "seen" and "appear." The unique secondary and profound spin on the sense of these terms is captured when we view manifest content as that which "appears" and latent content as that which is "seen," and that which appears is the words. The thing that is to be or can be seen is the latent content of the given words as we determine that content using a cipher technique such as an anagram. The reader must recall it is the original latent content that gives the word or the phrase its standardized outer form, and the form is based on a given key and reflects some hidden informational content. Ideas then are the invisible entities that inform what is seen in the above sense and can be traced by *studying* what is referred to as the seen. Hence, latent content embodies the actual popular wisdom. In other words, what mankind has rigorously established to be true wisdom is what the reader will find when the reader has acquired the aplomb to review latent content. Conceived in this way, one should then think of latent content as a "place" where *information* is stored. It is a *repository* especially catering to the refined popular wisdom and the related general dialogue. Consequently, developing an anagram from any type of written statement is like taking a snapshot of it by treating it like a piece of luggage to be x-rayed to determine its hidden content. What is seen, as latent content in an anagram, is most often not an accident. The information is deliberately placed and so it is socially constructed. In general, what is being stated then is that language, which necessarily is primed for cipher, is that which is created from facts. Those facts, as well-defined true technical and historical outcomes, are described in concise terms and then written in a shorthand which are thus made to assume the shape of the molds we call words. It is no real stretch of the imagination, and I am very comfortable in assuming, that the original meanings and descriptions of human actions were contained in letters alone. That is, it makes the most logical sense to believe whole word meanings or concepts were originally given as single letters of the alphabet.[1] After the above start, the recorded results of human activity have been borne in words as words. Hence, in both directions we see things-in-themselves. What we discover using the skill of ciphering by the technique of anagram are the popular facts already known and recorded by mankind. However, as I have repeatedly stated, in assigning ultimate responsibility to the Holy Spirit we cannot always perform the cipher and get into the latent content storehouse.[2] With respect to the depth and breadth of understanding, words are refractory in nature. Durkheim makes the above points clear, when he states:

> Indeed, the most important characteristic of a "thing" is the impossibility of its modification by a simple effort of the will. Not that the thing is refractory to all modification, but a mere act of the will is insufficient to produce a change in it; it requires a more or less strenuous effort due to the resistance which it offers, and, moreover, the effort in not always successful. We have already seen that social facts have this characteristic. Far from being a product of the will, they determine it from without; they are like molds in which our actions are inevitably shaped. This necessity is often inescapable. But even when we triumph over it, the opposition encountered signifies clearly to us the presence of something not depending upon ourselves. Thus, in considering social phenomena as things, we merely adjust our conceptions in conformity to their nature. (ibid., pp. 28–29)

Now the relevant question becomes, with all the information

embedded in cryptic form within language, how is mind or thought impacted as a whole by these molds we call words? The answer to that question is beyond the scope of this book.

The following key is made up of various characteristic entries. The primary entries are of the general type where words and letters are pre-assigned to the twenty-six (26) letters of the English alphabet. Another characteristic entry is where a single letter ends up occurring twice, and I use the pertinent word assigned to the particular letter being repeated, together with the word "is" to fulfill its contextual meaning. For example, the double letter "uu" would be assigned the word "you" to coincide with the letter "u," and then combined with the word "is" to form the two-word representation "you is" or "is you" to represent the double letter's definition. Still another key characteristic has been to assign words to letter combinations based on the "sound" generated or on phonetics, if you will. Finally, words have been assigned where an anagrammatic statement was begun yet a minimal number of amorphous residual letters remained, and based on the context, a few well-placed *additional* letters helped to complete the word or thought implied or suggested. The anagrams that have been based on this latter format I call "extensions," and some completed words of this type are exhibited, as a characteristic sampling, on the initial page of my anagram listings. Additionally, I have added parenthetical notes to assist the flow of meaning within individual anagrams. Thus the necessary and sufficient key for the given set of anagrams is as follows:

A all	N in
B be	O own, owe
C seem, "c," see	P people
D done, dumb, dark	Q
E he, me	R r = w,[3] ours, our, hours, are
F fucked, fast, "f," fuck	S yes, street
G game, "g"	T time

H him, how, her	U you
I me, eye	V v = f
J	W double you
K ok	X
L yell, tell	Y why, "Y," woman, women
M him, made, my	Z

Phonetic and shorthand entries:

def . . . deaf	bro . . . brother
yu . . . you	li . . . lie
han . . . hand	ma . . . may
dr . . . doctor	lex . . . lexicon
th . . . that	st . . . street, steak
im . . . I am	ez . . . easy
yo . . . flow	nite . . . night
at . . . after	bt . . . beat, bet
flo . . . flow	nd . . . need
ts . . . test	ss . . . secrets, secret service
gy . . . guy	zaid . . . said
waj . . . wage	wah . . . war
osa . . . oh say	nichel . . . nickel

Examples of the double letter form: uu   you is

uu	you is
cc	see is
nn	in is
etc.	

The above key should assist the reader in understanding how the following anagrams were individually developed, and how anagrams on this level are constructed generally. The fact some letters in the above key have not yet been assigned any word or additional letter value should offer no concern. The given key in an expanded or "grown" word and letters form would potentially have each letter with multiple word and letter assignments. What is significant is this minimal key can yield such a wealth of new information, as the reader can begin to glean from just the given anagrams. Lastly, before the reader begins experiencing this set of anagrams, I want to forewarn the reader, while these anagrams are not intended to offend anyone, these are adult topics and some items can be offensive to various individuals.

Learning is often a highly emotional enterprise, and this work by its very nature is a unique learning experience. So check out these anagrams and then hook up with me again in chapter five for some more dialogue.

(PART TWO)

And ye are witnesses to these things.

—Luk 24:48

Some Extensions		
Willa Ford	**A WOMEN'S THREAT**	Brown Sugar
dil[do]	men	s[h]rug
raw	sa[say]	bar
fo[o]l	throw	own
	eat	

MOUNT ETNA		Human Clone	Thank You for Having Me Y'all
tune	mat[h]	c[see]	k[ok]
no	no	name	honey
mat[h]	tune	hu[e]	hu[e]
		lo[a]n	talk
			for
			m[him]
			fay
			gain

ATTACKS	THE TRANSACTION OF OBEDIENCE		BEER
task	c[see]	c[see]	we
act	bid	bid	be
	action	action	
	e[he]	so	
	then	e[he]	
	want	then	
	o[own]	want	
	fee	own	

	so	fee	

Weather		Martin Lawrence	
w[double you]	w[double (cross) you]	law	law
eat	eat	win	win
her	her	men	men
		c[see]	e[he]
		e[he]	c[see]
		art	art

Thoughts About Freedom	Horror
we	wow
ought	how
be	
fast	
doom	
hut	

Terrorism		One World Order
term	wise	o[own]
is	m[him]	word
wow	tow	done
	r[ours]	l[yell]
		wow

Rooted Out		Monistat	The Case of the Tell-Tale Talk Show Host
toot	toot	tom[Uncle Tom]	hat
r[ours]	r[ours]	stain	theft
e[he]	e[he]		a
d[dumb]	d[done]		shock
			let
			tell
			how

			ease (easy)
			lost

Web of Deceit	Operation Noble Eagle	We're at War
CEO	eat	we
wife	I[me]	eat
debt	nope	r[ours]
	below	raw
	o[own]	
	angle	

Henry George	
e[he]	why
why	e[he]
Negro	G.E.
G.E.	Negro

Pontiac	Put Them Out of Business	Whatever	
p[people]	pest	few	wear
o[own]	but	hate	heft
act	sin	r[ours]	
I	mouth		
n[in]	o[own]		
	fuse		

Attack on America	Debra Burlingame
name	game
is	in

tactic	bed
all	u[you]
r[ours]	brawl
ok	

119

Luetrell Osborne	
e[he]	sue
born	lot
well	e[he]
lot	well[privileged]
sue	born

Maxine Waters	**Sweet baby**
sweat	we
win	by
me	beats
ax	

Osama Bin Laden					Diane Winkler
a	no	a	I	so	klan
sin	bad	lad	sold	me	win
me	sin	in	a	ban	we
loan	a[all]	so	bane	a	die
bad	lame	me	man	lad	
		ban		in	

The Hydrogen Atom: An Introduction to Representation Theory	Haverford College
why	have
truth	our
action	leg
wow	is
intent	cool
generate	def(deft)
tension	
mood	

today	
hope	

Lights, Camera, Action			
malice	great	lactation	white
has	action	came	lion
traction	h[he]	r[ours]	act
g	claims	sigh	a
			scam
			game

Raise Up	Evgeni Plushenko	We Right Here	
a[all]	feeling	we	wire
wise	poke	weight	her
up	h[he]	her	get
	n[in]		h[he]
	us		

Igor Lukashio	
I	I
law	go

skin	u[you]
u[you]	law
go	skin

Tian Liang		Aleksandr Variamov	Irina Lobecheva
a	n[in]	drama	achieve
gain	gain	so	win
lit	lai (defn)	flaw	o[owe]/[own]
n[in]	t[time]	fake	lab
		n[in]	

Show Me Where you Laid Your Brother Down	
there	yes

how	her
her	would

own	own
read	how

yes	you
you	read
would	there
my	my
bro[brother]	bro[brother]

Mohammed Atta		Wiretap Expansion
mm[him is]		war
tamed		a[all]
aa[all is]		p[people]
hot		exit
		pension

Ayub Ali Khan		Preparing for War
a[all]	yu[you]	we
yu[you]	be	p[people]
b[be]	a[all]	pawn
a[all]	k[ok]	grow
li[lie]	a[all]	fair
k[ok]	han[hand]	
han[hand]?!	li[lie]	

Eric Darton		**Gary Tuckman**	Richard Grasso	
note	I	many	so	I
I	draw	track	hard	c[see]

c[see]	"c"	u[you]		was	r[ours]
draw	note	g		I	was
				c[see]	so
				r[ours]	hard
				g	g

Order	Zaid Jarrah	Osama Bin Laden
wow	said[zaid]	osa[oh say]/U.S.A.
e[he]	wage[waj]	ma[may]

d[dumb]/[done]	war[wah]	b[be]
		in(internally)
		laden(burdened)

Emergency Medical Technician				Alexis On Fire	
rim	menace	agency	magician	o[own]	o[on]
agency	hit	c[see]	mercy	fine	is
hit	agency	decline	nichel[nickel]	is	fine
menace	c[see]	menace	end	relax	relax
c[see]	dim	hit	tee		
decline	recline	rim	c[see]		

Author: Harvey Kushner	Title: Future of Terrorism	Sylvana Soligon
he	wow	song
y[why]	is	lion
far	term	"f" [fucked]
knew	for	slay
us	uu[you is]	a[all]
	"f" [fucked]	
	e[he]	
	t[time] ("it" me)	

Peter Gold		Dr. Cheryl Arutt		Subject: Presburger Groups
got	go	dr[doctor]	Dr[doctor]	soup
deep	deep	c[see]	c[see]	burger
r[ours]	r[ours]	her	" y "	grew
I[yell]	tl[tell]	" y " [vagina]	her	p[people]?
		a[all]	a[all]	s[yes]!
		l[yell]	l[yell]	
		r[hours]	r[hours]	
		tt[time is]	tt[time is]	
		u[you]	u[you]	

Speaker: Richard Kaye	Edward Cardinal Egan	
key	dead	car
hard	" g "	n[in]
I	n[in]	"g"
wac(wack)	car	dead
	denial	denial
	war	war

Deepika Sarttalure	Omar Wasow
keep	wam (wham)
date	o [owe]
as	so
u[you]	war
r[ours]	
tail	

Pentbomb	Joe Lhota	
p[people]	jot	jot
be	a	o[own]
n[in]	hole	heal
tomb		

Alexander Degrand	Samuel Kassow	
lex[lexicon]	k[ok]	k[ok]
and	amuse	a
we	low	low
a[all]	ass	ass
grade		muse
n[in]		
d[dumb]/[done]		

Trinity College Professor of Italian Studies
city
wit
n[in]

profess
roof
e[he]
it
own

leg
I[yell]
stud
is
a
alien[UFO]

Author: Susan Zuccotti			Title: Under His Very Windows: The Vatican and the Holocaust in Italy
out	saint	s[yes]	h[he]
cuss	outs	cuss	do
saint	us	aint	win

	c[see]	out	dear!
			y[why]?
			hint:
			cause
			low
			friend
			has
			talent
			fist
			can
			hit
			you

Title: Silent No More: Confronting America's False Image of Islam
silence
is
a lame
front
o[own]
forgot
saga
mnemonics
fire
a[all]
mail

Title: Hitler, the War, and the Pope	
peep	peep
and	and
I[yell]	l[tell]
thwart	thwart
her	her
own	own

hit	hit

Hartford, Connecticut	**Earring**	
hard	win	gear
t[time]	gear	win
for		
i.d.		
cut		
connect		

Ear piercing	Payne Stewart	Emeril Lagasse	
I	pay	s[yes]	meal
creep	nest	sage	sage
a[all]	e[he]	wile	wiles
grin	war	meal	
	t[time]		

Author: John Hope Franklin	Title: My Life and an Era			
join	if	I	I	many
open	year	fear	fear	e[he]
hh[he is]	land	land	land	I[eye]
k[ok]	mean	y[why?]	e[he]	fear
ran		mean	many	land
f[fast]				

Happily Ever After	
happ	happy
y	
lie	lie
few	" f "

rate	rate[benefit]
" f "	few

Breath
we
b[be]
a[all]
th[that]

Dr. Jorge Piedrahita
what
died?
rape
r[ours]
I
jog

Ana Robar		Law and Order
o[owe]!	o[own]	law

a	ran	down
bar	a	a[all]
ran	bar	wed

Elvis Stojko	Johnny Weir		Alexei Yagudin	
list	why	why	exude	lay
of	coin	new	gain	I
jokes	[k]new	coin	I	exude
			lay	gain

Nail It Down and We've Got Motive
down
to
give
of
time…
nail(date),

ant(work),
wed

College: Salve Regina University		
law	see	safe
unity	virgin	virgin
see	safe	unity
virgin	law	law
safe	unity	see

College President: Sister Therese Antone		
see	the	st[street]
st[street]	wise	see
the	want	the
wise	one	wise
want	see	want
one(a virgin)	st[street]	one

Christina Otero	Mary Roosa	
choose	room	room
wine	was	" y "
wit	y[why]	was
t[time]	a[all]	a[all]

Complete Dell System		"Hello Mrs. Lindsey"
c[see]	sect [yes he see time]	hey
y[why]	let	Ms…
st[street]	me	d[dumb]
let	sell…	in
me	mop[my own people]	sell
sell	d[dumb]	low
mop	y[why]	

"You're not by any chance computer-shopping, are you?"

pry	(Citation: Dell Computer commercial)	
can		
come		
hoping		
you	**" She intriqued?"**	

buy	sin	he	
share	he	quit	
put	quit	wed	
note	wed	sin	
way			
one	**"Thanks Stephen"**		

c[see]	hen	hen	
	pest	step	
	th[that]	thanks	
	sank		

Phil Keoghan
hi
h[he]
n[in](created)
geo(the earth)
lap

Secretary			
secret	r[ours]	a[all]	a[all]
a[all]	a[all]	r[ours]	secret
r[ours]	secret	secret	" y "
y[why]	y[why]	" y "	r[ours]

Wanted		Check it Out
ant	wed	c[see]

wed	ant	heck
		it
		out

Alphonso Capone		Great
phone	(phony)	r[ours]
on	soap	eat
c[see]	on	g[game]
soap	c[see]	
a[all]	a[all]	
I[tell]	I[yell]	

Can You Stand to Be Great?
g[game]
r[ours]
bet
o[own]

and
you
can
eat
st[street] / [steak] / [yes time]

Anxiously Waiting to Be Deployed		Probably Means About Two and a Half Hours	
existing	existing	aha	aha
deed	deed	left	oh
only	only	doubt	left
ploy	ploy	ours	doubt
bait	bait	saw	ours
o[own]	you	woman	saw
a[all]	a[all]	baby	woman
u[you]	o[own]	plan	baby

Don't Say a Word			
don	st[street]	don	stay
way	don	road	down
road	roadway	st[street]	a[all]
st[street]		way	r[ours]
			do

Invectives			John Michelotti	
stiff	see	in	hit	Joe
see	in	see	lot	hit
in	stiff	stiff	him	lot
			c[see]	him
			Joe	c[see]
			n[in]	n[in]

Tom Sluiter	**Never Too Far**		Chadeen Palmer
to	few	few	law
m[him]	won	now	me
it	o[own]	o[own]	e[he]
slew	fate	fate	had
u[you]			c[see]
			pen

Glacier National Park
page
work
l[tell]
I
act
anal
in

Western Wildfires		
dire	news	if

news	dire	r[ours]
west	west	die

if	I[eye]	west
w[double you]	" f "	news
I[tell]	I[tell]	I[yell]
	w[double you]	w[double you]

Matt Rainy	Building		Bob Blau
ain't	lid	lid	blab
my	bug	bug[g]in	u[you]
tar / rat	in		B.O. (bad odor)

Newark	**Mark Seibel**		
wake	seem	bar	milk
r[ours]	I/[eye]	milk	be
n[in]	b[be]	see	e[me]
	lark		was

Amy Fickling	Dr. David Faxon	Heather Graham
many	now	eat
lick[beat]	did	her
fig	fad	hag
	fax	ham
		r[ours]

Lifetrack	What If	Love of My Life	
lift	faith	foe	fly
race	w[double you]	fly	me
k[ok]		me	foil
		foil	foe

I'm lookin'		Charles Payne
m[him]	ill	help
ill	m[him]	saw

no	no	c[see]

ok	ok	nay
		e[he]

Former Deputy Director of State Dept. Office of Counterterrorism	Training Day	
o[own]	grid	nay
foot	ain't	grid
error	nay	ain't
fate		
enter		
dispute		
come		
dry		
pit		
suffice		
from		
d[dumb]		
rector (school/church)		
t[time]		

Mary Schiavo	
I	fay
fay	so
so	I
charm	charm

C. Virginia Fields			
c[see]	c[see]	safe	lid
lid	virgin	lid	safe
I[eye]	lid	I	I
virgin	I	c[see]	c[see]
safe	safe	virgin	virgin

Wanted Dead or Alive			
live	want	oral	dan
read	dead	deed	t[time]
want	live	want	deal
o[own]	o[own]	a	adore
add	read	dive	wife
e[he]			

R i g h t G u a r d Deodorant		Victoria Toensing		Robert Crandall	
hard	hard	wait	fiction	down	down
order	order	fiction	wait	wall	wall
ain't	ain't	so	so	be	brat
do	rug	e[he]	e[he]	rat/tar	e[he]
t[time]	do	g[game]	" g "	c[see]	c[see]
gg["g" is]	t[time]	n[in]	n[in]		
u[you]					

Robert Butterworth	Crusade		Roger Porter	
we	ruse	cad	w[double you]	pow
wow	cad	ruse	we	wet
but			grew	o[own]
the			o[own]	grew
rot			pot	
time				
b[be]				
r[our]				
tow				

Amanda Grove	Fond Exit	
wave	fix	t[time]
a	t[time]	fix

d[dumb]		done	done
man			
go			

Aileen Sigany	Ceasefire		
glean	c[see]	ease / (easy)	fire
any	ease / (easy)	c[see]	ease / (easy)
II[I is]	fire	fire	c[see]
s[yes]			

Khaled Safouri		James Zogby		Sister Thy Brother Is Seated	
loud	hair	a	jog	rather	sis
hair	safe	mess	by	try	rather
safe	loud	jog	a	o[own]	try
k[ok]	k[ok]	by	mess	the	o[own]
				best	the
				sis	best
				side	side

Something in the Past		Inferior		Jack Zelmanowitz
past	past	fine	wow	jazz
e[he]	e[he]	I	I	man
thing	them	wow	fine	cloke
so	so			wit
them	Im[I am]			
Im[I am]	thing			

Fallin	Area Codes	Caramel
ill	does	law
fan	we	came
	c[see]	

	aa[is all]	

Obstetrics			Nabil Al-Marabh		Anjem Choudary Al-Mouajiroun	
wit	so	so	nab	a	major	major
st[street]	be	wit	m[him]	hall	name	name
c[see]	wit	be	a	Rab[b]i	could	is
be	st[street]	c[see]	hall	nab	join	why
so	c[see]	st[street]	Rab[b]i	m[him]	aa[all is]	you
					uu[you is]	could
					why	join
						is
						all

Hardball	California Love		Single White Glove
w[double you]	I	I	fog
bad	call	call	I[tell]
hall	own	own	sin
	if	if	we
	a[all]	a	hit
	foe	foe	glee

Confidence	Arabic		Pragmatism
c[see]	a	see	gramma
e[he]	Rab[b]I	a	tips
confide	c[see]	Rab[b]i	
n[in]			

White Cadillac	Donald Rumsfeld		
a[all]	Mad?	Mad?	fun
c[see]	s[Yes!]	Yes!	road

we	d[dumb]	found	smell
hit	found	well	dd[is done]
ill	well	done	
cad			

Operation Enduring Freedom			Zoolander
me	end	doom	so
end	we	ending	do
waiting	waiting	r[ours]	learn
proof	proof	free	
we	done	we	
done	u[you]	taping	
u[you]	me	u[you]	

Fly Fishing	The Next of Kin to the Wayward Wind	Better to Reign in Hell Then Serve in Heaven
if	he	weigh
shy	o[owe]	in
fling	kin	nerve
	text	then
	win	bet
	war	to
	font	win
	way	even
	he	heat
	is	sell
	time	
	done	

Why Should Christians Suffer
his
double

shy
her
furs
could
faint
you

Wish I Could Help You	Boys Choir of Harlem	Africa's Deadly Dozen	
why	yes	find	find
should	how	scar	scared
I	foil	a[all]	a[all]
clue	harm	dose	lay
p[people]	b[be]	delay	dose
I	o[own]		
o[own]	c[see]		
clue	harm	dose	lay
p[people]	b[be]	delay	dose
I	o[own]		
o[own]	c[see]		

Dmitri Kasterine	You Gets No Love			
d[dumb]	soft	golf	love	no
e[he]	guy	set	no	you
wink	tone	you?	set…	set
I	e[he]	no!	"g"	glove
master	I[tell]		you	
it	o[own]			

Rep. Porter Goss				Male Chauvinist Pig		
report	yes	yes	yes	a[all]	a[all]	you
we	is	is	we	c[see]	c[see]	see

p[people]	we	we	is	u[you]	u[you]	a
go	go	people	go	lip	hag	lip
ss[yes is]	report	go	report	hag	lip	hag
	people	report	people	feminist	feminist	feminist

Rep. Shelley Moore		Taliban				Fawzi Shobokshi	
more	more	t[time]	I	I	if	hh[he is]
he	pit	I	ban	tell	sis	if
eyes	eyes	I[yell]	a[all]	time	saw	sis
r[ours]	r[our]	ban	l[tell]	all	book	saw
pool	pool	a[all]	t[time]	ban	hh[he is]	book
I[yell]	I[tell]					
cap	a[all]					
it	[see]					

Sen. Max Baucus		Slowly		What It Is		
men	cuss	owl		shit	wit	it
b[be]	men	sly		wait	is	was
a[all]	b[be]			hat	hit	
u[you]	a[all]					
ax	u[you]					
cuss	ax					

Up to Isomorphism							
u[you]	must	top	most	show	up	I
miss	sip	soup	poor	us	to	too
him	ho[whore]	is	him	I	eye	am
too	Im[I am]	how	is	too	sore	wimp
pro	poor	Im[I am]	up	am	h[him]	so
" p "		m[him]		pimp	peep	push
					more	

					is	
					h[how]	

The Art of War	R.E.O. Speedwagon	Zeitgeist
a[all]	Negro	get
r[ours]	saw	it
thwart	e[he]	is
foe	dope	ez[easy]

"Where the Party At"				Sciences	Alexei Arbatov
here	ee[he is]	he	path	cc[see is]	I
we	threat	wet	art	I	abate
that	why	" y "	we	sense	or
party	trap	we	" y "		a[all]
		path	he		flex
		art	wet		

Howard Anton	Differences	
o[own]	fences	fence
no	if	if
hard	we	we
want	d[dumb]	d[dumb]
		s[yes]

Capital Punishment	Take You Out	Gideon Yago
pun	a[all]	day
meant	key	gig
I[yell] /l[tell]	out out [is out]	o[own]
I		one
cap		
shit		

Abuzed Omar Dorda (Libyan Ambassador)	Nasser Al-Kidwa (Palestinian Ambassador

141

drama	klan
abused	side
door	saw
	a[all]
	r[ours]

Globalization	Antonio Negri		Revolution
son	I	No?!	fool
gloat	ain't	ain't	e[he]
alibi	no	I	in

		Negro	Negro	rut		
Knock Yourself Out					Worst-Case Scenario	
u[you]	ok	so	loot	key	I	I
soft	NY	loot	fuck	run	can[stop]	can[dismiss]
our	u[you]	run	run	so	care	s[street]
key	felt	fuck	key…	fuck	so	so
in	our	key	so!	loot	s[street]	worst
lock	sock				worst	care

Universal	Universality	Delinquency in a Birth Cohort
I	it	e[he]
rule	y[why]	nab
fans	I	Quincy
	rule	wit
	fans	I
		lend
		how
		hot

		c[see]	

Nobody Has Our Sources				Theorem	
sour	boys	hours	sour	we	we
course	had	around	boys	o[own]	o[owe]
had	no	boss	had	them	them
no	sour	yo(flow)	no		
boys	source	e[he]	source		
		c[see]			

Name of the Rose				Foucault's Pendulum		
those	fore-name	name	for	those	soul	soul	soul
name	those	those	those	for	cult	cult	cult
e[he]		e[he]	e[he]	e[he]	map	map	map
for		for	name	name	fend	you	you
					uu[you is]	is	is
						fend	" f "
							end

Definitions			Notion	Abstract		
I	sit	i.e.	I	cab	bac[k]	star
sit	I	sit	no	stat	sta[b]	b[be]
find	find	on	into	r[ours]	r[ours]	act
on	one	find				
e[me]						

Tax-deferred Annuity				
try	nite[night]	try	" y "	any
wax	try	fee	refer	tit
fee	wax	wax	dude	n[in]
a[all]	fan	dd[dumb is]	at[after]	ax

dd[is done]	ee[he is]	a[all]	nn[is in]	refer
n[in]	dud	n[in]	taxi	dude

Exponential Functions		Elliptical Functions	Robert Tools (Artificial heart recipient)
exact	exact	lip	wow
point	point	fun	tools
one	sin	tells	be
I[yell]	fun	action	t[time]
sin	one	I	
fun	l[yell]	c[see]	

Alan Dershowitz			Try Again	
how	s[yes!]	ho	r[ours]	gay
we	we	slander	ain't	ain't
lands	sit	wits	gay	r[ours]
a[all?]...	a[all]	a[all]		
sit!	land			
	how			

Fermat's Last Theorem	
fast	fast
master	master
we	we
o[owe]	I[yell]
them	o[own](adopt, sponsor, support, and/or identify with)
l[tell]	them

"Fossett Aborts Balloon Mission, Lands in Brazil"	"Ballon Trip Aborted" (News Soundbite)	
born	trap	we

brazen		tool	trap!…

I		we	bail
floss		bail	bond
ballasts		bond	tool
I			
miss			
land			
I			
toot			
on			

Algebra					
grab	rage	leg	real	wage	we
ale	lab	a	gab	lab	b[be]
		bra			a
					gal

Abstract Algebra			
lab	t[time]	real	slab
wage	race	brat	act
tab	tabs	gab	tab
st[street]	lab	l[tell]	r[our]
car	rage	st[street]	rage
		c[see]	

Robert Hormats			
how	tame	t[time]	t[time]
tame	how	tame	robs
st[street]	t[time]	how	how
rob	robs	robs	r[hours]
r[ours]	r[ours]	r[ours]	tame

Moody Blues	Clive Cussler

me	dye	some	if
sold	mob	b[be]	cuss
o[own]	soul	y[why]	e[he]
buy		loud	c[see]
			well

Author: Alice Kaplan	Title: The Collaborator	The Door Is Open		
I	labor	tire	so	so
lack	e[he]	so	die	poor
a[all]	color	po oh	poor	die
e[he]/[me]	that	end	then	then
plan				

Film: "Along Came a Spider"			
lease	measle	I	l[tell]
can	can	d[done]	m[him]
go	go	rap	d[dumb]
m[him]	rapid	can	can
paid		go	go
r[ours].		l[tell]	I
		m[him]	rap
		easy	easy

Aces and Eights	Megan Rose	Never Be the Same Again
yes	same	saw
ace	Negro	a/a[all]
is		gain
nigh		then
date		fee

		be	

Alex Cross			
saw	saw	yes	c[see]
lex[lexicon]	lex[lexicon]	o[own]	saw
c[see]…	so	c[see]	lex[lexicon]…
so!	c[see]	saw	so!
		lex[lexicon]	

Rob Sobhani	Tiger Woods	Barry Bonds
be	wires	barn
o[own]	to	dry
is	God	so
how		b[be]
a[all]		
sin		

Tommy Hilfiger		Old Navy		You Know
my	home	d[dark]/d[dumb]	old	y[why]
gift	my	I[yell]	fay	o[owe]
home	gift	ofay	n[in]	u[you]
I	I	n[in]		k[ok]
I[tell]	I[yell]			now
r[ours]	r[hours]			

'Cause I Ain't Got No Money	Motherfucker	Our Assurance of Safety in Uncertain Times
c[see]	fume	you
gain	other	o[owe]
use	c[see]	me

meant	r[ours]	sin
o[owe]	k[ok]	ass
yin		is
too		certain
		you
		after
		fan
		cunt

Emotions and Relationships	God Can Hear the Blood
hips	hood
motions	bear
a[c]tions	gloat
we(gal)	he
land	c[see]
e[he]	n[in]

The Sound of Innocent Blood	Hick	Ayaz Amir	
o[owe]	h[he]	say	ours
inn	I	all	is
cent	c[see]	I	all
so	k[ok]	am	I
th[that]		is	am
blood		ours	say
e[he]			
found			

Al-Qaeda		Barnett Rubin	Receiving
leada[leader]	cue	bar	we
q[cue]	all	bet	c[see]
a[all]	is	nut[cum]	g[game]
	deal	win	I
			fine

There's No Finish	Hodja Bahaudeen	Rush Out and Get Some	
wish	do	use	o[own]
those	a[all]	grant	me
n[in]	u[you]	o[owe]	d[dumb]
fine	had	shout	grant
	been	me	use
	Haj	d[dumb]	shout

Muhammad Atef		
a[all]	fame	a[all]
math	math	mud/dum[b]
fame	dum[b]/mud	math
mud/dum[b]	a[all]	fame

I Think			Fuck	
h[he]	it	ink	" f "	f[fuck]
ink	h[he]	It	u[you]	u[you]
it	ink	h[he]	c[see]	k[ok]
			k[ok]	c[see]

Twenty Biblical Principles for Debt Release	
Bible	Bible
people	people
wince	wince
went	if
be	call
as	went
if	be
s[yes]	witty
ditty	as
call	r[ours]?
is	d[dumb]
ours	s[yes]!

It's About Going Out with the Band And Doing Your Own Thing		
ban	ban	ban
doing	doing	doing
your	your	your
out	out	out
thing…	thing…	thing…
go	go	go
with	with	with
it	it	it…
then	then	then
guts	su[e]	dad
in	boating	guts
b[be]	dad	in
a[all]		b[be]
o[own]		a[all]
		o[own]

Homeland Security Swearing In	On My Way	
in	no	" y "
swear	way	is
to	m[him]	woman
secure	"y" /why	
land		
him		
yin		
g[game]		

Harry Potter and the Chamber of Secrets by J.K. Rowling			
Table of Contents			
The Worst Birthday	Dobby's Warning	The Burrow	
story	sing(music)	bt[bet]/[beat]	hue
be	yarn	hue	bt[beat]/[bet]

width	bow	r[ours]	r[ours]
thaw	b[be]	wow	wow
	d[dumb]		

At Flourish and Blotts			
that	flo[flow]	at[after]	float
s[o]ot	at[after]	flo[flow]	u[you]
is	u[you]	u[you]	wish
flour	wish	wish	a[all]
bland	a[all]	a[all]	nd[need]
	nd[need]	nd[need]	blot
	Blot	blot	ts[test]
	ts[test]	ts[test] (Rorschach Test)	

The Whomping Willow	Gilderoy Lockhart		Mud Bloods and Murmurs
who	gild	gild	sum
willing	we	we	land
pow	yo/[flow]	lock	woods
them	lock	h[e]art	rum
	h[e]art	yo[flow]	dumb

The Death Day Party		The Writing on the Wall		
hey	death	th[r]ew	tie	wall
dear	day	wit	in	tie
day	they	in	th[that]	in
tt[time is]	part	th[that]	the	th[that]
path		wall	wrong	the
		gone	wall	wrong

The Rogue Bludger		The Dueling Club	The Polyjuice Potion
there	rude	thing	tie

151

u[you]	go	due	o[own]
go	there	b[be]	joy
lug	b[be]	l[tell]	punch
be	lug	clue	top/pot
r[are]			lie
d[dumb]			

The Very Secret Diary	Cornelius Fudge		Aragog
the	I[eye]	I[eye]	aa[all is]
cry	clone	fuse	r[ours]
fey	d[dumb]	clone	own is g [game]
see	rug	d[dumb]	
wart	fuse	rug	
I.D.			

The Chamber of Secrets	
Crete	Crete
thef[t]	thef[t]
bar	bar
me	c[see]
c[see]	ho
h[he]	mess
o[own]	
ss[secrets]/	
secret service	

The Heir of Slytherin				Dobby's Reward	
the	their	their	he	boys	boys
sly	flo[flow]	o[own]	o[own]	r[ours]	r[hours]
win	y[why]	fly	fly	be	be
fe[e]	he	he	s[yes]	dd[dumb is]	dd[done is]

their	win	win	their	war	war
ho	the	the	the		
	s[yes]	s[yes]	win		

J.K. Rowling		Harry Potter	
owl	c[see]	Why	why
King	wink	pot?	we
c[see]	low	We	to
r[ours]	g[game]	art!	part

The Protestant Ethic and the Spirit of Capitalism	
t[time]	he
he	protest
protest	ant
ant	ethic
ethic	n[in]
n[in]	d[done].
d[done] . . .	tt[is time]
t[time]	he
he	wit
wit	own,
o[only]	if
f[first]	man
capital	list(key)
is	capa[ble].

m[made]

Nuclear Energy	
n[In] (Inside)	

u[you]	
clear	
e[he]	
new	
gy[guy] (and/or woman)	

"Understanding Elementary Algebra with Geometry: A Course for College Students"	
understand	understand
my	my
gallery	gallery
brats	brats
colleagues	colleagues
he	wit

wanting	force
wit	wanting
force	he
or	or
tee(peg)	tee(peg)
men	men
e[we]	e[we]
geo(the earth)	geo(the earth)
stud	stud

Lord of the Rings: The Two Towers	
how	world
world	hint
sting	goes:
h[her]	f[fuck]
foe	the
to	two
sweet	towers

r[our]	
t[time]	

Frank Sinatra
" F "
ranks
in
r[ours]
at[after]
a[all]

ENDNOTES

1   Any discussion of "numbers" as word and cipher are reserved for future discussions under a separate cover.

2   There are two excerpts from the King James Version of the Bible that are pertinent to this discussion. They are John 1:1 and John 4:24. The one tells us God is word and the other tells us God is spirit, respectively. If we accept what these verses say to us, then we have no recourse but to conclude word is spirit and spirit is word. And as we are led to experience it in real time, the Holy Spirit does reveal intricacies of itself—word—to us.

3   The equation r = w is a very significant finding. My observation that the letter r, in the cipher of the general lexicon, is more often than not a stand-in for the letter w has significance even beyond my own immediate comprehension. I find it not insignificant that the letter w, phonetically pronounced "double you," literally helps to double the meaning content of the lexicon once it is appropriately substituted for the letter. Thus the letter r is one of the keys to the larger alphabetical key that I have supplied.

CHAPTER FIVE

GOD ONLY KNOWS?!

And they shall not teach every man his neighbour, and every man his brother, saying, Know the Lord: for all shall know me, from the least to the greatest.

—Heb. 8:11

The examples in the previous chapter have now had a chance to speak for themselves. And the above quote gives credence to why I have, as previously mentioned, no need to proselytize. All I need to do is present a fair and objective representation of reality, which is my primary hope. To that continuing effort, this chapter is directed toward some biblical content, which I believe is essential to our understanding. I am not a biblical scholar, so I will limit my comments to what I feel most comfortable with in regard to this wisdom. Ergo, the reader will have to use his/her own judgment as to what he/she feels is acceptable (Rom. 12:2). In that connection, I will also address the issue of faith.

As I understand the original scenario that is related biblically, God the father, God the son, and God the holy spirit, at some point, had a conversation in heaven about a new creation called "man." God the father explained his desire to make man in the flesh and in his own image. However, he knew that if he created man, man would betray his trust and thereby fall from his grace, and that behavior on the part of man would anger God the father. When man would disappoint God

157

the father in the above manner, God's wrath would be provoked and that would be sufficient for him to destroy man, and he did not want to create something that he would be obliged to destroy. God the father thus needed a remedy for this inevitability before he could create man.

God the son then intervened with a resolution by volunteering to be the sacrifice himself on behalf of man to appease God the father's anger when man had fallen from grace. God the son agreed to assume a human form, live a blameless life of faith in God the father, innocently give up the life in the flesh, and then, given God the father's grace, to conquer death. God the son agreed to do all of this under the condition God the father would return him to his seat at the father's right hand in heaven, and that he would become the sole mediator for man with God the father. That is, once his mission was completed, if anything would be asked by man of God the father, first in the name of God the son, it would be granted to them. Thus God the father, through his grace and mercy, made a covenant with God the son. It was a blood covenant. Consequently, God the son would have to assume a human form, made possible by God the father, and shed his blood and die, before the covenant would be fulfilled. In other words:

> In the beginning was the Word, and the Word was with God, and the Word was God. The same was in the beginning with God. All things were made by him; and without him was not anything made that was made. In him was life; and the life was the light of men. And the light shineth in darkness; and the darkness overcame it not. (Joh 1:1–5)

Of course, there are several layers of meaning in the above quote. The level of meaning that is important for our immediate purposes would be interpreted as follows: "In the beginning was the Word." There was a discussion—an exchange of words—going on in heaven concerning things already known about what was yet to come into existence. "And the Word was with God." God the Son, who was present with God the Father, gave his word, made a promise to be the sacrifice to God the Father for man. "And the Word was God." The Holy Spirit, who was also present with God the Father, was God the Word or the word God. For the Bible says: "God is a Spirit: and they that worship him must worship him in spirit [word] and in truth [belief in his son]" (Joh 4:24). Those of us who reach to the higher wisdom will appreciate that the word truth in the last quote refers to the combined effect of God the Father and God the Son's agreement or covenant with regard to man. There was no doubt they would be true to their own word! It is truth with the intensity of the notion of an absolute reality. Moreover, the reader should come to understand the Holy Spirit has a special status in the triad of the Godhead. Thus the Holy Spirit would also have a unique role to play with regard to the sustenance of man, and I will discuss the role of the Holy Spirit shortly.

As for his part, having fallen from grace because of having committed a pivotal sin, man would have to first believe in Jesus the Christ, God the Son's earthly name, before he would be saved. And this without exception:

> Because that which may be known of God is manifest in them [man]; for God hath shown it unto them. For the invisible things of him [God] from the creation of the world are clearly seen, being understood by the things that are made [his word, including the Bible], even his eternal power and Godhead, so that they are without excuse. (Rom 1:19–20)

And since God is Word, man would be obliged to express his belief, verbally, in words. According to Romans:

> But what saith it? The word is nigh thee, even in thy

mouth, and in thy heart: that is, the word of faith. . . .
That if thou shalt confess with thy mouth the Lord Jesus,
and shalt believe in thine heart that God hath raised him
from the dead, thou shalt be saved. For with the heart
man believeth unto righteousness; and with the mouth
confession is made unto salvation. For the scripture saith,
Whosoever believeth on him shall not be ashamed. . . . So
then faith cometh by hearing [understanding and accepting
or believing], and hearing by the word [content of the Bible]
of God. (Rom 10:8–11, 17)

So the open vocal confession of one's belief is the test of whether
or not one's spirit is or is not of God. The Bible implores us, and it is
unequivocal on this point:

Beloved, believe not every spirit, but test the spirits
whether they are of God: because many false prophets
are gone out into the world. Hereby know ye the Spirit of
God: every spirit that confesseth that Jesus Christ is come
in the flesh is of God: And every spirit that confesseth not
that Jesus Christ is come in the flesh is not of God: and
this is that spirit of antichrist, whereof you have heard that
it should come; and even now already is it in the world.
Ye are of God, little children, and have overcome them:
because greater is he [Spirit] that is in you, than he [flesh]
that is in the world. They are of the world: therefore speak
they of the world, and the world heareth them. We are of
God: he that knoweth God heareth us; he that is not of
God heareth not us. Hereby know we the spirit of truth,
and the spirit of error. (1 Joh 4:1–6)

Therefore those who do not believe also act in and as a spirit, but
theirs is the spirit of "error" and not the spirit of "truth." Moreover, a

believer immediately becomes a member of the family of believers, who too are assured, through faith, the original covenant made by God the father and God the son has been fulfilled. As St. Paul suggests:

> Wherefore I also, after I heard of your faith in the Lord Jesus, and love unto all the saints, cease not to give thanks for you, making mention of you in my prayers; that the God of our Lord Jesus Christ, the Father of glory, may give unto you the spirit of wisdom and revelation in the knowledge of him: The eyes of your understanding being enlightened; that ye may know what is the hope of his calling, and what the riches of the glory of his inheritance in the saints, and what is the exceeding greatness of his power to us-ward who believe, according to the working of his mighty power, which he wrought in Christ, when he raised him from the dead, and set him at his own right hand in the heavenly places. Far above all principality, and power, and might, and dominion, and every name that is named, not only in this world, but also in that which is to come: and hath put all things under his feet, and gave him to be head over all things to the church, which is his body, the fullness of him that filleth all in all. (Eph 1:15–23)

Before Jesus's arrival on earth much had been prophesized about his imminent arrival and subsequent activities, according to God the father's overall plan for the salvation of man. As it was prophesized:

> Behold my servant, whom I have chosen; my beloved, in whom my soul is well pleased: I will put my spirit upon him, and he shall shew judgment to the Gentiles. (Mat 12:18)

Upon his arrival on earth, Jesus received this power of the Holy Spirit granted by God the father. He went about the land using the power of the Holy Spirit to make moral judgments, to physically heal individuals among the gentiles, the non-chosen, and to apprentice his disciples. The Pharisees (Jewish clergymen) followed Jesus around and were disturbed by all the good Jesus was doing for the gentiles, so they challenged him whenever they believed they had the opportunity. In fact, the Bible relates repeated occurrences where, upon observing the activities of Jesus, and challenging him to his face, "the Pharisees went out, and held a council against him, how they might destroy him" (Mat 12:14). Now there came a time when Jesus had had enough of at least one level of their harassment when the Pharisees had the audacity to verbally profane the source of his power, the Holy Spirit, the Word. Jesus expressed his indignation in making it clear the Holy Spirit held a special status within the Godhead, and it was not to be defiled. As the Bible relates the incident:

> Then was brought unto him one possessed with a devil, blind, and dumb: and he healed him, insomuch that the blind and dumb both spake and saw. And all the people were amazed, and said, Is not this the son of David? But when the Pharisees heard it, they said, this fellow doth not cast out devils, but by Beelzebub the prince of the devils. And Jesus knew their thoughts, and said unto them, every kingdom divided against itself is brought to desolation; and every city or house divided against itself shall not stand: And if Satan cast out Satan, he is divided against himself; how shall then his kingdom stand? And if I by Beelzebub cast out devils, by whom do your children cast them out? [Jesus appears here to be eluding to his possible maligned legacy's potential impact on future generations of children and to the fact that like the Pharisees he too was born a Jew. Additionally, he is saying that when the Pharisees own children cast out devils they were exhibiting similar behavior.] therefore they shall be your judges [He

is saying that he considers the Pharisees to be devils too].
(Mat 12:22–27)

As a consequence of his being able to read *their thoughts*, we observe here that Jesus provides a counter argument to their accusations. He unequivocally emphasizes the severity of their words by expressing how, in the future, loose comments of this nature would not be without consequence. As he further observes:

> But if I cast out devils by the Spirit of God, then the Kingdom of God is come unto you. Or else how can one enter into a strong man's house, and spoil his goods, except he first bind the strong man? and then he will spoil his house. He that is not with me is against me; and that gathereth not with me scattereth abroad. Wherefore I say unto you, All manner of sin and blasphemy shall be forgiven unto men: but the blasphemy against the Holy Ghost [giving Satan credit for what the Holy Ghost had done] shall not be forgiven unto men. And [furthermore] whosoever speaketh a word against the Son of man [against Jesus himself], it shall be forgiven him: but whosoever speaketh against the Holy Ghost, it shall not be forgiven him, neither in this world, neither in the world to come. (Mat 12:28–32)

Jesus refused to allow the Pharisees or anyone else to defile his dominion by attributing the good they saw him doing to evil intent. We know this because he went on to say:

> Either make the tree good, and his fruit good; or else make the tree corrupt, and his fruit corrupt: for the tree is known by his fruit. O generation of vipers, how can ye [Pharisees] being evil, speak good things? for out of the abundance of the heart the mouth [what we really feel in

our hearts is easily discerned by what we say] speaketh. A good man out of the good treasure of the heart bringeth forth good things: and an evil man out of the evil treasure bringeth forth evil things. But I say unto you; That every idle word that men shall speak, they shall give account thereof in the day of judgement. For by thy words thou shalt be justified, and by thy words thou shalt be condemned. (Mat 12:33–37)

One should begin to notice that the Bible is unequivocal in its statements. For example, when discussing the confession of belief in Jesus the Christ, one is either a believer or possesses the spirit of the Antichrist. In the immediate comments above, Jesus admonishes the Pharisees to call things one thing or the other but not to hedge. Of course, an emphasis on the importance and power of words permeates the entire Bible. One must recall that God is Word! In fact, the Word as God is so deeply Word it even reaches to the letters in words as Word. As one writer puts it:

For which cause we faint not; but though our Outward [manifest content] man [as physical body] perish, yet the inward [latent content] man [as spirit] is renewed day by day for our light affliction [our inability to always immediately see where we are going with our lives or know what we are doing], which is but for a moment, worketh for us a far more exceeding and eternal weight of glory; while we look not at things which are seen, but at the things which are not seen: for the things which are seen are temporal; but the things which are not seen are eternal (2 Cor 4:16–18)

Man is made in the image of God. Thus, our essence is Spirit or Word. Consequently, the above sense in which I use the term man is synonymous with Word. The idea I am suggesting here is somewhat abstract and uncommon or atypical with respect to its meaning; and, perhaps, can only be appreciated as one begins to understand how the concept of faith must be applied. "For we walk [we continue from here] by faith, not by sight" (2 Corinthians 5:7).

At this point, it would be appropriate for us to define faith, but let us pause for a moment and complete our point about meaning and word and meaning in the word as related to the depth of meaning inherent in the very letters of words. One must appreciate it is God's will that we truly understand his word. And at this level, the understanding of words becomes the most sensitive of explanations because personalities and routinely taken-for-granted habits of thought can get in the way of our understanding. The Bible expresses the ideas as follows:

> For though I should boast somewhat more of our Authority [our knowledge of words and the power and authority contained in word meanings], which the Lord hath given us for edification, and not for your destruction, I should not be ashamed [like minority students reportedly being ashamed of learning]; That I may not seem as if I would terrify you by letters. For his letters, say they, are weighty and powerful, but his bodily presence is weak, and his speech contemptible. Let such an one think this, that, such as we are in work by letters [literally] when we are absent[generations of thinkers and educators, now deceased, who have passed the information and its understanding on], such will we be also in deed when we are present. [They are saying that their words will have an impact on actual future reality. That is, through words they are helping to create what will be observed physically in the future.] For we dare not make ourselves of the number [we are not coming to you with abstruse material like mathematics or with boasting of what as individuals or groups of individuals we

have done], or compare ourselves with some that commend themselves among themselves, are not wise [theirs is real power and not bravado]. (2 Cor 10: 8–12)

The writer is explaining that those who truly understand and act using God's word do not feign their understanding or couch it in narrow—opinionated—perspectives and gloating, or smug and insular posturing. The writers in this group recognize, if the reader is denied the opportunity to or is truly unable to understand what words are meaning, the effect is that the reader becomes intimidated or worst terrified by the words. The above type of writer wants to do everything within his/her power to prevent such a potentially destructive outcome. It is virtually impossible for the avid reader to not notice the appearance of subtle meanings in the usage of words. Therefore instead of attempting to attribute their deeper understanding merely to their own innate ability, writers of the above caliber attribute all their knowing to its real source and that is God. For the writer continues:

But we will not boast of things without [outside of] our measure, but according to the measure of the rule which God hath distributed to us, a measure to reach even unto you [the boaster and deceiver]; for we are come as far as to you also in preaching [people reaching or proselytizing, not for self- aggrandizement but for the furtherance of] the gospel of Christ, Not boasting of things without our measure, that is, of other men's labors [for that is what the mean-spirited and deceitful do], but having hope, when your faith is increased, that we shall be enlarged by you [believing if we help teach you that you and yours will in turn teach us and our posterity] according to our rule abundantly, to preach the gospel in the regions beyond you, and not to boast in another man's line of things made ready to our hand [not narrowly within any pre-established field of study or discipline]. But he that glorieth, let him glory in the Lord. For not he that commendeth himself is approved, but whom the Lord commendeth [for works given us through the holy spirit]. (2 Cor 10:13–18)

It is important that one does not misunderstand what is being stated here. These scriptures are not suggesting one cannot or should not study any particular field of learning known to man, but, rather:

Of these things put them in remembrance, charging them before the Lord that they strive not about words to no profit, but to the subverting of the hearers [being deliberate in your effort to influence the listeners mind towards thoughts consistent with God's will for all of us to understand his word. And not to use what are actually his words to deliberate confuse and misled others.] Study to show thyself approved unto God, a workman that needeth not to be ashamed,[1] rightly dividing [explaining, uncovering, and revealing, etc. . . . in all disciplines] the word of truth. (2 Tim 2:14–15)

For when it is stated that God is word, it literally means every word written about anything, anywhere, at any time, and in any language or form belongs to God. And the Bible suggests we should submerge ourselves in every form of word, for example, science, poetry, art, and music. The Bible states:

Let the word of Christ dwell in you richly, in all wisdom teaching and admonishing [advising] one another in psalms [rhymes, operas, ballads, and rap] and hymns [instrumentals, jazz, classical music, chants] and spiritual songs [gospel music] singing with grace in your hearts to the Lord. And whatever you do in word or deed, do all in

the name of the Lord Jesus, giving thanks to God and the
Father by him. (Col 3:16–17)

Perhaps now the reader can more readily understand why even "rap"
artists often publicly give thanks and praise to God for their work and
their success during music award ceremonies. No doubt they too are
aware that their words as song lyric have a higher calling. You must
begin to understand that every word in any context that is uttered at any
time belongs to God and is ultimately uttered for his divine purpose.
We come closer to appreciating these things as we understand and grow
in faith: "but [first understand] the wisdom that is from above is first
pure, then peaceable, gentle, and easy to be intreated [sic], full of mercy
and good fruits, without partiality, and without hypocrisy" (Jas 3:17).
That is correct! What many so-called religious folks would refer to as
secular, believe it or not, is also part and parcel of God's word domain.
For "the kingdom of heaven is like to a grain of mustard seed, which a
man took and sowed in his field: which indeed is the least of all seeds;
but when it is grown, it is the greatest among herbs, and becometh a
tree" (Mat 13:31–32). And a tree typically has many diverse branches!

Many might criticize me and call the above comments outrageous,
"But [the Bible says] I beseech you, that I may not be bold when I am
present with that confidence, with which I think to be bold against some,
who think of us as if we walked according to the flesh. For though we
walk in the flesh, we do not war after the flesh. For the weapons of our
warfare [the words we use from the most holy to vile invectives] are not
carnal, but mighty through God to the pulling down of strongholds.
Casting down imaginations, and every high thing that exalteth itself
against the knowledge of God, and bringing into captivity every thought
to the obedience of Christ" (2 Cor 10:1–5). The average person is full
of opinionated ideas about matters of fact in his/her everyday life.
People more often than not are too intellectually lazy to delve into the
complexity of the matters before them. Consequently, people easily

and frequently allow their opinions, about both public and private matters, to lead them to rush to judgments about others and what others do, without the benefit of the better informed or correct and complete set of facts.

> But why dost thou judge thy brother [fellow man]? Or why dost thou set at nought [disregard, dispise, and discriminate against] thy brother? for we shall all stand before the judgement seat of Christ. For it is written, as I live, saith the Lord, every knee shall bow to me, and every tongue shall confess to God. So then every one of us shall give account of himself to God. Let us not therefore judge one another any more: but judge this rather, that no man put a stumblingblock [deliberately cloud the pathways to immediate clear thinking] or an occasion to fall in his brother's way [player hate…practice acts of jealousy and discrimination]. I know, and am persuaded by the Lord Jesus, that there is nothing unclean of itself: but to him that esteemeth anything to be unclean, to him it is unclean. But if thy brother be grieved with thy meat, now walkest thou not charitably. Destroy not him with thy meat, for whom Christ died. Let not then your good be evil spoken of. (Rom 14:10–16)

The last point made in the above quote is most important. It suggests we should constantly be mindful of the fact that our actions can negatively affect others and rather than make bad situations worst, we should seek to remedy untoward situations as *best we* can. "And [it is written] I, brethren, could not speak unto you as unto spiritual, but as unto carnal, even as unto babes in Christ. I have fed you [in the past] with milk, and not with solid food; for to [before] this time ye were not able to bear it, neither yet now are ye able. For ye are yet carnal; for whereas there is among you envying, and strife, and divisions, are ye not carnal, and walk as men?" (1 Cor 3:1–3)

It is certainly clear that not everyone is prepared to dispense or to receive this level of knowledge, but here too the Bible has a word for us:

> Thou therefore, my son, be strong in the grace that is in Christ Jesus. And the things that thou hast heard of me among many witnesses, the same commit thou to faithful men, who shall be able to teach others also. Thou therefore endure hardness, as a good soldier of Jesus Christ. No man that warreth entangleth himself with the affairs of this life; that he may please him who hath chosen him to be a soldier. And if a man also strive for masteries, yet is he not crowned, except he strive lawfully. The husbandman that laboureth must be first partaker of the fruits. (2 Tim 2:1–6)

The above quote suggests that we should be eager to listen to the faithful who demonstrate their understanding. We should also be willing to teach those who believe but who do not fully understand. It should be obvious that those individuals who are always merely at war with the affairs of this world do not truly understand God's word. However, do not waste time badmouthing others. One should handle one's own affairs and the other affairs with which one is directly involved in in the conventional world constructively and trust God to take care of the rest that is his own business. That is, do not trivialize the fight! Always do things humbly in faith and in the name of Jesus Christ. Then and only then is one in the appropriate state of mind to receive the perfect reward of understanding promised in God's Word, and, after that, one who believes will begin to taste the fruits of one's faith, so it is said:

> And I was with you in weakness, and in fear, and in trembling. And my speech and my preaching was not with enticing words of man's wisdom, but in demonstration of

the spirit [spy wit] and of power [owe our people]: That your faith should not stand in the wisdom of men, but in the power of God [owe our people God food]. Howbeit we speak [yes peak (reach the highest point of the)] wisdom among them that are perfect: yet not the wisdom of this world, not of the princes of this world, that come to nought: But we speak the wisdom of God in a mystery, even the hidden wisdom, which God ordained before the world unto our glory: Which none of the princes of this world knew: for had they known it, they would not have crucified the Lord of glory. But as it is written, eye hath not seen, nor ear heard, neither have entered into the heart of man, the things which God hath prepared for them that love him. (1 Cor 2:3–9)

And the statement continues:

But God hath revealed them unto us by his spirit: for the Spirit searcheth all things, yea, the deep things of God. For what man knoweth the things of a man, save the spirit of man which is in him? even so the things of God knoweth no man, but the Spirit of God. Now we have received, not the spirit of the world, but the spirit which is of God; that we might know the things that are freely given to us of God. Which things also we speak, not in the words [formal education] which man's wisdom teacheth [albeit formal education is also to be received], but which the Holy Ghost teacheth; comparing spiritual things with spiritual. But the natural man receiveth not the things of the Spirit of God: for they are foolishness unto him: neither can he know them, because they are spiritually discerned. But he that is spiritual judgeth all things [words as social facts], yet he himself is judged of no man. For who hath known the mind of the Lord, that he may instruct him? But we have the mind of Christ. (1 Cor 2:10–16)

So then, to them who are spiritual:

Unto you it is given to know the mysteries of the kingdom of God: but to others in parables [anagrams if you will]; that [because] seeing they might not see, and hearing they might not understand. Now the parable is this: The seed is the word of God. Those by the way side are they that hear; then cometh the devil, and taketh away the word out of their hearts, lest they should believe and be saved. They on the rock are they, which, when they hear, receive the word with joy; and these have no root, which for a while believe, and in time of temptation fall away. And that which fell among thorns are they, which, when they have heard, go forth, and are choked with cares and riches and pleasures of this life, and bring no fruit to perfection. But that on the good ground are they, which in an honest and good heart, having heard the word, keep it, and bring forth fruit with patience. No man, when he hath lighted a candle, covereth it with a vessel, or putteth it under a bed; but setteth it on a candlestick, that they which enter in may see the light. For nothing is secret, that shall not be made manifest; neither any thing hid, that shall not be known and come abroad. Take heed therefore how ye hear: for whosoever hath, to him shall be given; and whosoever hath not, from him shall be taken even that which he seemeth to have. (Luk 8:10–18)

From these quotations, we understand that the Holy Bible is the seed and it is the word of God. Moreover, "the sower soweth the word" (Mar 4:14). However, although it may be available to us, the Bible is

172

not so easily understood. While the Bible does delineate all and more of the details of what I am explaining in this book, without faith it is literally impossible to truly understand the Bible. Faith is the main ingredient of a complete understanding of God's word. The biblical writer Paul demonstrates that he understands the relationship of faith and spirit, when he tells us:

> For Christ sent me not to baptize, but to preach the gospel: not with the wisdom of words, lest the cross of Christ should be made of none effect. For the preaching of the cross is to them that perish foolishness; but unto us which are saved it is the power of God. [The power one receives from this simple act of faith in Christ crucified.] For it is written, I will destroy the wisdom of the wise, and will bring to nothing the understanding of the prudent. Where is the wise? where is the scribe? where is the disputer of this world? [God had planned it all beforehand . . . before man had a chance to have any say or part in it at all.] hath not God made foolish the wisdom of this world? For after that [after God had planned it all] in the wisdom of God the world by [its version of] wisdom knew not God, [and knowing these untoward outcomes even before time began] it pleased God [that is, God decided] by the foolishness of preaching to save them that believe. (1 Cor 1:18–21)

Although formal education is necessary and essential to this level of understanding, no amount of book-based learning will be sufficient to perfect this understanding. And here, in what immediately follows, is where one must be careful not to misunderstand what is being said but, rather, understand what is being said in light of what was just stated above. We return here to the paradoxical notion of dangerous thoughts when we read:

For ye see your calling, brethren, how that not many wise men after the flesh, not many mighty, not many noble, are called: but [or because] God hath chosen the foolish things of the world to confound the wise; and God hath chosen the weak things of the world to confound the things which are mighty; And base things of the world, and things which are despised [for example curse words], hath God chosen, yea, and things which are not, to bring to nought things that are. (1 Cor 1:26–28)

What is obvious from the above statements is that it is impossible to know what the complete and active will of God is, as we set out to have our behavior conform to his will. All we can really know for sure is our part, and that is we must confess our belief in the scenario of Christ crucified [his birth, life, crucifixion, and resurrection] and we will be saved. Being saved means being able to interpret and use what we individually learn from the Holy Spirit, and to know behavior that is in agreement with the correct interpretation can potentially put us, as individuals, in compliance with God's will for our lives. We are also informed:

There is nothing from without a man that entering into him can defile him: but the things which come out of him, those are they that defile the man. If any man have ears to hear, let him hear. And when he [Jesus] was entered into the house from the people, his disciples asked him concerning the parable. And he saith unto them, are ye so without understanding also? Do ye not perceive, that whatsoever thing from without entereth into the man, it cannot defile him…and he said, that which cometh out of the man, that defileth the man. For from within, out of the heart of men, proceed evil thoughts, adulteries, fornications, murders, thefts, covetousness, wickedness, deceit, lasciviousness, an evil eye, blasphemy, pride, foolishness: all these things come from within, and defile the man. (Mark 7:15–18, 20–23)

So we must be mindful of and sensitive to what is in our hearts. Since what we mentally ingest through various media will necessarily affect our inner thoughts, we must be careful not to permit unwelcome thoughts to passively mold our being and thus negatively inform our actions. And no one knows the heart of another person but God. This is the reason we should not be so high-minded that we think we can rightfully make routine moral judgements on others.

However, we are encouraged, even in our own frailty, to assist others. That is:

> Brethren, if a man be overtaken in a fault, ye which are spiritual, restore such an one in the spirit of meekness, considering thyself, lest thou also be tempted [to act stupidly]. Bear ye one another's burdens, and so fulfil the law of Christ. For if a man think himself to be something, when he is nothing, he deceiveth himself. But let every man prove his own work, and then shall he have rejoicing in himself alone, and not in another. For every man shall bear his own burden. Let him that is taught in the word [clergy] communicate unto him that teacheth in all good things [educators]. Be not deceived; God is not mocked; for whatsoever a man soweth, that shall he also reap. For he that soweth to his flesh shall of the flesh reap corruption; but he that soweth to the Spirit shall of the Spirit reap life everlasting. And let us not be weary in well doing: for in due season we shall reap, if we faint not. (Gal 6:1–9)

Thus, we have before us a multiplicity of facts and beyond that only faith. But what is this faith of which we speak? The Bible is very explicit in defining faith:

> Now faith is the substance of things hoped for, the evidence of things not seen. For by it the elders obtained a good report [the facts such as they exist]. Through faith we understand that the worlds [the limits of all possible experience] were framed by the word of God, so that things which are seen were not made of things which do appear. By faith Abel [Able] offered unto God a more excellent sacrifice than Cain [someone who creates trouble or makes a disturbance—as in raise cane], by which he obtained witness that he was righteous, God testifying of his gifts: and by it being dead [Abel having been slain by Cain] yet speaketh [God's testimony being his legacy]. By faith Enoch [Enough] was translated that he [he- art] should not see death; and [death] was not found, because God had translated him: for before his translation he had this testimony, that he pleased God. But without faith it is impossible to please him: for he that cometh [testifies] to God must believe that he is, and that he is a rewarder of them that diligently seek him. (Heb 11:1–6)

It should by now be obvious to the reader that as the writer of this book, I believe in the life, crucifixion, and resurrection of Christ. And I have come this far in the depth and breadth of my exposition by an understanding based on faith. No doubt, it is clear what the ultimate purpose is of faith. Now we need to get some sense of the power of faith.

Jesus gave us a valued impression of the awesome power of faith in a response he gave to a request by the apostles: "and the apostles said unto the Lord, Increase our faith. And the Lord said, If ye had faith as a grain of mustard seed, ye might say unto this sycamine tree, Be thou plucked up by the root, and be thou planted in the sea; and it should obey you" (Luk 17:5–6).

Moreover, at another time he says: "For verily I say unto you, that whosoever shall say unto this mountain, be thou removed, and be thou cast into the sea; and shall not doubt in his heart, but shall believe that those things which he saith shall come to pass; he shall have whatsoever he saith. Therefore I say unto you, what things soever ye desire, when ye pray, believe that ye receive them, and ye shall have them" (Mar 11:23–24). So then: "be anxious for nothing, but in everything, by prayer and supplication with thanksgiving, let your requests be made known unto God. And the peace of God, which passeth all understanding, shall keep your hearts and minds through Christ Jesus" (Phi 4:6–7). Additionally, we are shown that true faith literally puts a demand on the power of God. We see this in the following example where:

> A certain woman, which had an issue of blood twelve years, and had suffered many things of many physicians, and had spent all that she had, and was nothing bettered, but rather grew worse, when she had heard of Jesus, came in the press behind, and touched his garment. For she said, If I may touch but his clothes, I shall be whole. And straightway the fountain of her blood was dried up; and she felt in her body that she was healed of that plague. And Jesus, immediately knowing in himself that virtue [some power] had gone out him, turned him about in the press, and said, Who touched my clothes? And his disciples said unto him, thou seest the multitude thronging thee, and sayest thou, Who touched me? And he looked round about to see her that had done this thing. But the woman fearing and trembling, knowing what was done in her, came and fell down before him, and told him all the truth. And he said unto her, Daughter, thy faith hath made thee whole; go in peace, and be whole of thy plague. (Mar 5:25–34)

Still, it is left to be determined the role and importance of faith in one's making contact with the Holy Spirit. For it is said:

> This only would I learn of you, received ye the Spirit by the works of the law, or by the hearing of faith? . . . For as many as are of the works of the law are under the curse: for it is written, Cursed is every one that continueth not in all things which are written in the book of the law to do them. But that no man is justified by the law in the sight of God, it is evident: for, The just shall live by faith. And the law is not of faith: but, the man that doeth them shall live in them. Christ hath redeemed us from the curse of the law, being made a curse for us: for it is written, Cursed is every one that hangeth on a tree. (Gal 3:2, 10–13)

Now we are informed that it is faith that provides the environment for the Holy Spirit to come upon us and not the old biblical law. As it is further explained:

> The scripture hath concluded all under sin, that the promise [of salvation] by faith of Jesus Christ might be given to them that believe. But before faith came, we were kept under the law, shut up unto the faith which should afterwards be revealed. Wherefore the law was our schoolmaster to bring us unto Christ, that we might be justified by faith. But after that faith is come, we are no longer under a schoolmaster. For you are all children of God by faith in Christ Jesus. . . . There is neither Jew nor Greek, there is neither bond nor free, there is neither male nor female: for ye are all one in Christ Jesus. (Gal 3:22–26, 28)

God's word says that by possessing the appropriate element of faith, one enters into a more peaceful emotional state than before.

"For we are made partakers of Christ, if we hold the beginning of our confidence stedfast unto the end; while it is said, to day if ye will hear his voice, harden not your hearts, as in the provocation. For some [utterances] when they had heard did provoke" (Heb 3:14–16). And the point continues: "Let us therefore fear, lest, a promise being left us of entering into his rest, any of you should seem to come short of it. For unto us was the gospel preached, as well as unto them; but the word preached did not profit them, not being mixed with faith in them that heard it. For we which have believed do enter into rest, as he said, As I have sworn in my wrath, if they shall enter into my rest: although the works were finished from the foundation of the world . . . and they to whom it was first preached entered not in [to the rest] because of unbelief . . . Let us labour therefore to enter into that rest, lest any man fall after the same example of unbelief. For the word of God is quick, and powerful, and sharper than any two-edged sword, piercing even to the dividing asunder of soul and spirit, and of the joints and marrow [body], and is a discerner of the thoughts and intents of the heart. Neither is there any creature [even symbolic monsters][2] that is not manifest in his sight: but all things are naked and opened unto the eyes of him with whom we have to do" (Heb 4:1–3, 6, 11–13).

Once we have studied to know and to understand it becomes clear that there is no reason why we should not remain strong in our faith. Through faith, our eyes are opened: "Seeing then that we have a great high priest, that is passed into the heavens, Jesus the Son of God, let us hold fast our profession. For we have not an high priest which cannot be touched with the feeling of our infirmities; but was in all points tempted like as we are [that is, Jesus empathizes with us because he has experienced what we are experiencing], yet without sin. Let us therefore come boldly unto the throne of grace [belief and faith], that we may obtain mercy, and find grace to help in time of need" (Heb 4:14–16). And furthermore we know "sin shall not have dominion over you: for you are not under the law, but under grace" (Rom 6:14). That is, our faith is sufficient to address any of our earthy needs.

Finally, I believe the following quote expresses what I believe has been my calling as relates to the production and the content of this book. My calling has not been to nullify or to malign the Greek tradition but, rather, to be contrasted with the tradition while maintaining a partnership with the Greek tradition. That is, rather than mystify, I have acted to demystify these matters. Both traditions have an invaluable place in the exposition of knowledge. The Bible amply expresses my approach as follows:

> Therefore seeing we have this ministry, as we have received mercy, we faint not; but have renounced the hidden things of dishonesty, not walking in craftiness, nor handling the word of God deceitfully; but by manifestation of the truth commending ourselves [our unusual understanding] to every man's conscience [one's personal understanding] in the sight of God. But if our gospel [go spell] be hid, it is hid to them that are lost [low street]: in whom the god of this world hath blinded the minds of them which believe not, lest the light of the glorious gospel of Christ, who is the image of God, should shine unto them. For we preach not ourselves, but Christ Jesus the Lord; and ourselves your servants for Jesus' sake. (2 Cor 4:1–4)

My book has only lain the foundation for the reader's potential excursion and growth in these mysteries. The real work and benefits can now begin and is left to the reader. Therefore it will be in the reader's interest to follow biblical advice, and "study to show thyself approved unto God, a workman that needeth not to be ashamed rightly dividing [reducing] the word of truth" (2 Tim 2:15).

ENDNOTES

1   The following anagram is suggestive of the meaning in context of the word:

Ashamed

e [we]

d [done]

a

sham

2   In his classic book entitled *Proofs and Refutations*, Imre Lakatos refers to any pathological element in a mathematical proof as a "monster." Moreover, because of the nature of his work and his particular genius, I feel the above book by Lakatos would be interesting data for study by way of ciphering.

CHAPTER SIX

NOW THAT WE KNOW?!

*For I tell you, that many prophets and kings have desired to see
these things which ye see [as I am showing them to you], and have
not seen them; and to hear those things which ye [now are able, so
to speak, to] hear, and have not heard them.*

—Luk 10: 24

My intention in this chapter is to make a few of what I consider
to be important general and summary comments. Of course
it is likely that some readers will consider the comments
provocative and even controversial. No matter, in view of all that I have
already outlined in this book I feel obliged to state the case that there
are some serious phenomena existing in our world and remaining to
be explained. With that in mind, my initial comment is that this is
not a book on religion. That is, although I value all religions, it is not
my intention in this work to advocate any particular religion. In the
last chapter, I did not actually talk about religion per se, but rather, I
necessarily discussed belief and faith within the context of religion. In
my opinion, it is only incidental and a consequence of my personal
biography that the path I am taking in discussing the current "stock
of knowledge" is through Christianity. One needs keys to unlock the
mysterious, and who is to say definitively what are the limits of how
the keys can be and are to be originally forged. However, I would not
hesitate to claim that both language and its keys are divinely conceived.

182

I have also wanted to point out and to confirm, for those individuals who believe there are hidden messages in song lyrics, commercial messages, news sound bites, names, and other written materials, that they are correct. The good news is that reader's who fall into the above group now have a direct method of discerning some sense of what is actually written there. One is able to discern these things by means of the technique of ciphering. The literary expressions of the above types of statements are especially vulnerable to analysis via the technique of anagram derivation. Of course, there are numerous other cryptographic techniques that I could have shared that would extend the reader's skill in ciphering. But this is also not a book on cryptographic technique per se. However, the singular concept of anagram is well defined and helps to keep the neophyte investigator or researcher's feet on the ground, and being grounded to a tangible thing is something that is crucial when one is new to this mode of learning. In fact, had I not discovered the utility of the anagram, in the above regard, I might have elected not to publish this book. That is, as a technique, the anagram is reasonably safe with respect to not overwhelming people with technical abstractions, while at the same time routinely and consistently serving to yield meaningful tidbits or increments of information.

What one generally finds hidden in the above statements, by means of an anagram's derivations, is a lot of information and direct candor with regard to issues and events, feelings, and opinions on every imaginable topic, as opposed to some nefarious mind control devices. To bear witness to this fact, one need only review the anagrams in chapter four above. I believe the reason for the comfort with regard to the original candor is the fact that the statements are hidden from obvious popular consumption, yet paradoxically are not ultimately hidden. And that is a truth known to all those who utilize this particular venue for disseminating information. Although one has to adjust to some very hard facts in this realm of information, I am happy to report, I am finding there is by far many more good things than inherently evil things happening in our world, as is revealed in these esoteric literary and linguistic locations.

Ciphering literature is seeing life as a review of a continuous or never-ending motion picture. The motion picture does have a master plan, but one can only review the scenes a few frames at a time. Happily, however, one can in fact obtain an overview of the total picture by simply reviewing a sufficient number of cryptic segments of it. The result will be that the reviewer will discover the motion picture is all about the facts in and of life in general, and has application to the reviewer's own life in particular. Additionally, it is discovered that the more the reviewer ciphers the more the reviewer will learn about the above aspects of life. The interesting paradox of one's ability to cipher, as exemplified in my personal experience, is while I am formally educated and currently by vocation an educator, I suddenly find myself a very "slow learner" within the total scheme of things. That is, popular wisdom has already refined what I only relatively recently have discovered and begun learning more about. It is important to me that the reader recognizes and appreciates introspectively that what I have been attempting in this work, to the best of my knowledge, has not ever been publicly shown in such an explicitly open manner before.

The most important point to be made is that everything an individual thinks and says, which is the very substance of his/her individual identity, has consequences in his/her everyday life. Additionally, because we all live within the symbolic universe of discourse referred to as the" ether," what we think and say affects the lives of others in real time, and even future generations of people.[1] The idea mimics what medical science has discovered in recent years about the effects of secondhand cigarette smoke on the general population. Within the "ether" even our given names have significance. As a consequence, spiritual mediators exist in our present everyday world, in real time, who are privy to our personal transcripts, because they are empowered to hear what we ourselves think or speak and also to literally see what we write. They have the power to then make the desired and/or needed adjustments to affect an overall balance in the system, the ether, with an eye toward system maintenance, order, future planned growth, and progress. They accomplish this by their knowing what to do to alter or adjust the system—ether—itself, in order to be in compliance with the above divine agenda for society. It is my understanding that these characteristic individuals and entities collectively refer to themselves as "Eye."[2] Again let us be clear, as bizarre as it may sound, these beings or entities who are mediators are privy to our thoughts and spoken word, and all the while they also possess the power to literally see through our very own physical eyes. Because it is possible for others to "hear" our thoughts, they can know them and stay a step ahead of us and openly "mock" us. The mockery can be most irritating and even stultifying. If mockery is experienced, it can and should be ignored.

These are some of the characteristic phenomena that have existence in our world. They are among the true mysteries! To my knowledge, the phenomena mentioned here are not provable by conventional methods so most people would dismiss discussion of them as pure delusion, fantasy, mythology, illusion, or fiction. The reality of their actual existence really is incredible! However, those readers who will believe and come to the knowledge and the understanding through true "sensibility" will necessarily come to experience and thereby be able to know the existence of these phenomena. Of course, the one sense of knowing the phenomena being used here means, how is the phenomenon actually being accomplished? What are the laws of physics, radio waves, and electromagnets that make the phenomenon possible? I do not believe this sense of "how" is knowable even by most of those chosen, and who possess the capability to use the phenomenon. I believe that individuals are merely given possession of the powers to see and to hear, along with the wisdom to use the powers appropriately. On the other hand, the how and nature of the everyday life "mysteries" or the "mysterious," as evidenced by the content of the present book, can generally be known to a large extent. These more tangible mysteries address the age-old popular wisdom and our general stock of knowledge and not the above phenomena as such. Berger and Luckmann provide us with a more formal rendition of what I am saying here when they write: Identity is ultimately legitimated by placing it within the context of a symbolic universe. Mythologically speaking, the individual's "real" name is the one given to him by his god. The individual may thus "know who he is" by anchoring his identity in a cosmic reality protected from both the contingencies of socialization and the malevolent self-transformations of marginal experience [being socially and intellectually underprivileged]. Even if his neighbors do not know who he is, and even if he himself may forget in the throes of nightmare, he can reassure himself that his "true self" is an ultimately real entity in an ultimately real universe. The gods know, or psychiatric science, or the party [the state] (Berger and Luckmann, 1966, p. 93).

So individuals should not delude themselves in the belief that they are not looked after or watched over, and that when of age even their untoward activities are not known and monitored once arriving in the world. As Berger and Luckmann go on to observe:

> In other words, the *realissimum* of identity need not be legitimated by being known at all times by the individual; it is enough, for purposes of legitimation, that it [the real character of the individual—within an acceptable margin of error] is knowable. Since the identity that is known or knowable by the gods, by psychiatry, or the party is at the same time the identity that is assigned the status of paramount reality, legitimation again integrates all conceivable transformations of identity with the identity whose reality is grounded in everyday life in society. Once more, the symbolic universe [what one says—in the

186

aforementioned relevant forms] establishes a hierarchy, from the "most real" to the most fugitive self-apprehensions of identity. This means that the individual can live in society with some assurance that he really is what he considers himself to be as he plays his routine social roles, in broad daylight and under the eyes of significant others. (ibid.)

Who one is really is known even if one does not completely know oneself. Moreover, who we are as an individual is ultimately dependent on what we are "assigned" to be, and our lives are simply mediated constraining us to come into conformity with the divine assignment. Although very profound, the immediate comments above do not represent a definitive explanation but merely an overview of what the phenomena are about.

This is not some children's book and despite my effort to clarify and moderate its intellectual intensity, this book is not bedtime literature. Even with my best efforts to simplify these complex and subtle concepts, the intricacies of these complex ideas are observed to increase or "expand" indefinitely. This observation about the complex is the very nature and the profundity of the substance we are investigating. Many of the points being made here are very subtle, and that is both by necessity and by design. While on the one hand claiming his work was a manual [Immanuel as in "I'm or I am manual"] on these matters, Kant [as in "cant" or "jargon"] also claimed these topics could never be made ready for popular consumption.[3] I have tried to prove Kant wrong. Whether or not I have succeeded in my effort to make the foregoing ideas more palatable, can only be ultimately decided by my book's readers. No matter, I believe I have accomplished at least one thing. That is, on the face of it, and if one considers past practice, the present exposition has made the intellectual and technical playing field fairer. If I have succeeded in at least helping to make the playing field fair, then that is all I could realistically have hoped to accomplish. The world and society presents us as individuals with an awesome reality that existed before each of us was born.

The mastery, on this level, of the basic realities of everyday life and the pertinent factual materials related to it has its basis in and is dependent upon a strong need or desire to know, in whichever way that is construed. The reason being that mastery of these matters and materials is very much dependent on the extent of one's formal exploration or exposure to the knowledge. Even if one does not choose to aspire to the mastery of a particular formal field of study or technical expertise, mastery of the affairs of everyday life and of the information being disseminated in everyday life necessitates hard work. That is to say, a lot of study and concentrated meditation is required for its mastery. Obviously, on his/her individual journey, I have chosen to wish the traveler well.

ENDNOTES

1   Of course, the reader should be advised there is a molecular or quantum interpretation and discussion of the ether that is beyond the scope of this book.

2   My insight into this informal appellation is a result of the information issuing from my extensive study of informal "information technology" and its content, using techniques of the type mentioned in my book. I should remind the reader that if he/she were to look at the back of any one dollar bill in United States currency there would be found a triangle, and at the top of that triangle a triangulated eye. Moreover, to the right of that triangle and over the word "one" will be found the words: "In God we trust." The average person would likely take this symbolism for granted or attribute little significance to it. There could even be some readers of the present book who would characterize the above symbols as mere coincidence. This latter group would be among those who have not read my book with discernment. Lastly, let the reader be clear about what I have not said in this regard. I did not say that "Eye" is to be considered synonymous with the federal government. What we are discussing here is slightly more complex than that.

3   A meaningful translation of this essential anagram within context is as follows:

Immanuel Kant

I

am

cant [jargon]

manual

References

Berger, Peter L. <u>Invitation to Sociology: a humanistic perspective</u>. New York: Doubleday and Company, 1963.

Berger, Peter L., and Thomas Luckmann. <u>The Social Construction of Reality: a treatise in the Sociology of Knowledge.</u> New York: Doubleday and Company, 1966.

Berkson, William. <u>Lakatos one and Lakatos two: an appreciation.</u> (From <u>Essays in Memory of Imre Lakatos</u>: Boston Studies in the Philosophy of Science. Ed. R. S. Cohen et al. (Vol. 39)). Boston: D. Reidel Publishing, 1976.

Bodanis, David. A <u>Biography of the World's Most Famous</u> Equation: E = MC2. New York: Berkley Publishing Group, 2000.

Bohm, David. <u>The Special Theory of Relativity</u>. 1965. New York: Routledge, 1996.

Boyer, Carl B. <u>A History of Mathematics</u>. 2nd ed. New York: John Wiley and Sons, 1968.

Durkheim, Emile. <u>The Rules of the Sociological Method</u>. 1938. 8th. ed. Trans. Sarah A. Solovay and John H. Mueller. New York: The Free Press, 1966.

Einstein, Albert. <u>Relativity: The Special and General Theory</u>. 1920. Trans. Robert W. Lawson. New York: Dover Publications, 2001.

The World As I See It. 1956. Trans. Alan Harris. New Jersey: Carol Publishing Group, 1999.

Sidelights on Relativity. 1922. Trans. G.B. Jeffrey and W. Perrett.

New York Dover Publications, 1983.

Foucault, Michel. Madness and Civilization: a history of insanity in the Age of Reason. London: Tavistock Publication, 1961.

Freud, Sigmund. On Dreams. Trans. James Strachey. New York:

W.W. Norton and Company, 1952.

The Interpretation of Dreams. New York: Avon Books, 1965

Sexuality and the Psychology of Love. 1963. New York: Simon and Schuster, 1997.

Gardner, Martin. Codes, Ciphers and Secret Writing. New York: Dover Publication, 1972.

Gerth, Hans and C. Wright Mills. Character and Social Structure: the psychology of social institutions. New York: Harcourt, Brace, and World, 1964.

Hayakawa, S. I. Language in Thought and Action. 1939. New York: Harcourt, Brace and Company, 1941.

Heath, Sir Thomas L. ed. The Method of Archimedes: recently discovered by Heiberg. Cambridge: Cambridge University Press, 1912.

Hegel, Georg Wilhelm Friedrich. Hegel's Science of Logic. Trans.

A. V. Miller. New Jersey: Humanities Press International, 1969.

Holsti, Ole R. <u>Content Analysis for the Social Sciences and Humanities</u>. Philippines: Addison-Wesley Publishing Company, 1969.

Johnson, Wendell. People in Quandaries: the semantics of personal adjustment. New York: Harper and Brothers, 1946.

Kant, Immanuel. <u>Critique of Pure Reason</u>. 1929. Trans. Norman Kemp Smith. New York: St. Martin's Press, 1965.

Lakatos, Imre. 1976. <u>Proofs and Refutations: The logic of mathematical discovery</u>. ed. by John Worrall and Elie Zahar. Cambridg: Cambridge University Press, 1995.

Leibniz, Gottfried Wilhelm. <u>Discourse on Metaphysics; Correspondence with Arnauld; Monadology. 1902</u>. Trans. George Montgomery. Illinois: Open Court Publishing, 1994.

Long, Calvin T. <u>Elementary Introduction to Number Theory.</u> 3rd. ed. New Jersey: Prentice Hall, 1987.

Mannheim, Karl. <u>Ideology and Utopia: an introduction to the Sociology of Knowledge</u>. Trans. Louis Wirth and Edward Shils. New York: Harcourt, Brace, and World, 1936.

Matza, <u>David. Becoming</u> Deviant. New Jersey: Prentice-Hall, 1969.

Merton, Robert K. Social Theory and Social Structure: revised and enlarged edition. Illinois: The Free Press, 1957.

Miliband, Ralph. <u>The State in a Capitalistic Society</u>. New York: Basic Books, 1969.

Mills, C. Wright. The Sociological Imagination. New York: Oxford University Press, 1959.

Sociology and Pragmatism: The higher learning in America.

New York: Oxford University Press, 1966.

Newton, John. Amazing Grace. Arr. by Norman Johnson. (From Carrell and Clayton's Virginia Harmony, 1831). 8th ed. New National Baptist Hymnal. Nashville: Triad Publications, 1977.

Ogden, C. K. and I. A. Richards. The Meaning of Meaning: a study of the influence of language upon thought and of the science of symbolism. New York: Harcourt, Brace, and World, 1923.

Polanyi, Michael. Personal Knowledge: towards a post-critical philosophy. 1958. London: Routledge and Kegan Paul, 1962.

Rieff, Philip. Freud: The Mind of the Moralist. New York: Doubleday and Company, 1959.

Scofield, C. I. ed. The New Scofield Study Bible. New York: Oxford University Press, 1967.

(Unknown editors). The Holy Bible. New York: The World Publishing Company, (unknown publication date)

Tarde, Gabriel. The Laws of Imitation. 1903. 2nd. ed. Trans.

Elsie Clews Parsons. Massachusetts: Peter Smith, 1962.

Tarski, Alfred. Introduction to Logic: and the methodology of deductive sciences. 1941. New York: Dover Publications, 1995.

Weber, Max. <u>The Protestant Ethic and the Spirit of Capitalism.</u>

Trans. Talcott Parsons. New York: Charles Scribner's Sons, 1958.

About The Author

Larry Odell Johnson is an assistant professor of mathematics at Dutchess Community College, where he has focussed on teaching lower-level mathematics courses for thirteen years. Those courses include beginning algebra through pre-calculus and statistics. A graduate of Arizona State University and U.C. Berkeley, Larry has degrees in mathematics and criminology. This is his first book, but he has previously published several articles in the academic journal *Issues in Criminology*.

When his is not teaching, Larry's interests include reading, fishing, music, movies, dancing, golf, and traveling.

Recently Larry was awarded Emeritus Status by the Board of Trustees at Dutchess Community College. He took his early retirement in 2004 and pursued a career in writing and research.

www.ingramcontent.com/pod-product-compliance
Lightning Source LLC
Chambersburg PA
CBHW032055020426
42335CB00011B/345